THE CLASSIC RECIPES OF ASIA

THE CLASSIC RECIPES OF ASIA

FRESH TASTES FROM THE FAR EAST WITH 100 TEMPTING DISHES SHOWN IN 300 STEP-BY-STEP PHOTOGRAPHS

SALLIE MORRIS AND DEH-TA HSIUNG

southwater

This edition is published by Southwater, an imprint of Anness Publishing Ltd,
Hermes House, 88–89 Blackfriars Road, London SE1 8HA; tel. 020 7401 2077; fax 020 7633 9499

www.southwaterbooks.com; www.annesspublishing.com

If you like the images in this book and would like to investigate using them for publishing, promotions or advertising,
please visit our website www.practicalpictures.com for more information.

UK distributor: Book Trade Services; tel. 0116 2759086; fax 0116 2759090; uksales@booktradeservices.com;
exportsales@booktradeservices.com
North American distributor: National Book Network; tel. 301 459 3366; fax 301 429 5746; www.nbnbooks.com
Australian distributor: Pan Macmillan Australia; tel. 1300 135 113; fax 1300 135 103; customer.service@macmillan.com.au
New Zealand distributor: David Bateman Ltd; tel. (09) 415 7664; fax (09) 415 8892

Publisher: Joanna Lorenz
Managing Editor: Linda Fraser
Project Editor: Mariano Kälfors
Designer: Nigel Partridge
Photography: Nicki Dowey
Food for Photography: Becky Johnson
Production Controller: Christine Ni

ETHICAL TRADING POLICY

Because of our ongoing ecological investment programme, you, as our customer, can have the pleasure and reassurance
of knowing that a tree is being cultivated on your behalf to naturally replace the materials used to make the book you
are holding. For further information about this scheme, go to www.annesspublishing.com/trees

© Anness Publishing Ltd 2000, 2010

A CIP catalogue record for this book is available from the British Library.

Previously published as *Fresh Tastes of Asia*

Main front cover image shows Duck Breasts with Pineapple and Ginger – for recipe, see page 32.

NOTES
For all recipes, quantities are given in both metric and imperial measures and, where appropriate, in standard cups and spoons.
Follow one set of measures, but not a mixture, because they are not interchangeable.
Standard spoon and cup measures are level. 1 tsp = 5ml, 1 tbsp = 15ml, 1 cup = 250ml/8fl oz.
Australian standard tablespoons are 20ml. Australian readers should use 3 tsp in place of 1 tbsp for measuring small quantities.
American pints are 16fl oz/2 cups. American readers should use 20fl oz/2.5 cups in place of 1 pint when measuring liquids.
Electric oven temperatures in this book are for conventional ovens. When using a fan oven, the temperature will probably need to
be reduced by 10–20°C/20–40°F. Since ovens vary, you should check with your manufacturer's instruction book for guidance.
Medium (US large) eggs are used unless otherwise stated.

PUBLISHER'S NOTE
Although the advice and information in this book are believed to be accurate and true at the time of going to press, neither the authors
nor the publisher can accept any legal responsibility or liability for any errors or omissions that may have been made nor for any
inaccuracies nor for any loss, harm or injury that comes about from following instructions or advice in this book.

CONTENTS

INTRODUCTION   6

CHINA AND HONG KONG   10

MALAYSIA AND SINGAPORE   38

THAILAND AND BURMA   58

INDONESIA   78

VIETNAM AND THE PHILIPPINES   94

JAPAN AND KOREA   108

SHOPPING FOR ASIAN FOODS   124

INDEX   126

INTRODUCTION

SOME OF THE WORLD'S most exciting cuisines come from the Far East and South-east Asia. From the vastness of China to the island states of Indonesia and the Philippines, food is prepared with pleasure and keen attention to detail. Each of the countries in this broad sweep has its own unique style of cooking. Coloured by climate, local crops, cultural customs and the impact of historical events such as invasion or war, each nation has its own culinary uniqueness, but there are common threads too. Throughout this region, the emphasis is always on serving food that is as fresh as possible. Presentation is paramount, particularly in Japan and Thailand, and the sharing of food is so fundamental to the faith of each culture that honoured guests are precisely that.

Below: Asia is a vast region, from China, through Japan and Korea, down to the South-east Asian islands of Malaysia, Indonesia and the Philippines.

Rice is the staple food of the whole of this region. Although wheat – in the form of noodles – is eaten more often than rice in some parts of Asia, such as northern China, Asians everywhere regard wheaten food as mere

Above: Patna rice is one of many types of long grain rice.

Right: Short grain japonica rice is ideal for sushi because, when cooked, the grains stick together.

Above: Basmati rice is a slender long grain rice grown in northern India. It has a cooling effect on hot and spicy curries.

supplements. Cultivated in southern Asia for more than five thousand years, rice is eaten at every meal, including breakfast, and is the basis of both sweet and savoury snack foods, as well as being a source for both wine and vinegar. Throughout Asia, the importance of rice is underlined by the fact that in Chinese and other Asian languages, there is no single word for rice, but many. The crop, grain, raw rice and cooked rice are all referred to by different terms, and the Chinese character *fan* for cooked rice has acquired a much wider meaning in colloquial speech; it is also synonymous with nourishment and good health. When friends meet, instead of asking "How do you do?" they will often greet each other with the words: "Have you eaten rice?" An affirmative answer indicates that all is well.

There are more than 40,000 different strains grown in China alone. Since rice requires a wet and warm climate for its

Fish is also an important part of the diet. Every country, with the exception of Laos, has miles of coastline, as well as rivers, lakes and ponds, all of which yield plentiful supplies of fish. The lower reaches of the Yangtze River are traditionally known as the "Land of Fish and Rice", a term that is used to indicate the well-being of the local inhabitants. The first king of Siam expressed similar sentiments when, in 1292, he wrote of the value of having "fish in the water and rice in the field".

The Japanese cooks' skill in preparing and serving fish is legendary. This is partly due to the fact that the country has abundant fish stocks and only limited land for grazing, but is also because for many years, meat was off the menu, due to a government decree that prohibited its consumption by any but the sick, on the grounds that it increased aggression. As a result, Japanese cooks became extremely adept at preparing fish in a wide variety of ways. Very fresh fish is sliced thinly and served raw, or marinated, but this is by no means the only way of preparing it.

Above: Exotic fish, such as snapper, parrot fish and pomfret are eaten widely throughout Asia.

cultivation, some 90 per cent of the world production of rice is grown (and consumed) in the monsoon regions of Asia. A small amount of rice is cultivated on dry land in northern China, but because of the cold climate, only one crop can be grown each year, whereas two crops per annum is the norm in the temperate south.

The most common way of serving rice throughout Asia is simply boiled or steamed; fried rice does not normally form part of an everyday meal, but is either served as a snack on its own, or reserved for a special occasion such as a banquet. Unlike the India pilau, the Italian risotto or the Spanish paella, Asian fried rice dishes are never based upon raw rice, but always use ready cooked rice (either boiled or steamed). For the finest results, the rice should be cold and firm, rather than soft.

The universal breakfast in all Asian countries is a creamy, moist rice dish, which is known as congee or rice pudding. Highly nutritious, it is often given to babies and people with digestive problems as well as the elderly. Coconut milk is used instead of water in many South-east Asian countries, but because it usually takes more than an hour to make a smooth, creamy congee, many cooks cheat by simply adding hot water to cold cooked rice.

Right: Tuna steaks and salmon cutlets are delicious barbecued or pan fried.

In Thailand, too, fish is of enormous importance. As elsewhere in Asia, it is always served as fresh as possible. In restaurants, it is usual for diners to choose their own fish from tanks, a serious business that demands considerable deliberation, and nobody objects to waiting while the grouper or snapper is despatched, prepared and cooked in the manner the diner has selected. Fish bought at market is often live and is carried home in a bucket of water for preparation by the cook.

The Asian preoccupation with the freshest possible food, be it animal or vegetable, can be a little disconcerting for the Western visitor. Before enjoying the famous Hong Kong dish Drunken Prawns, for instance, the diner must first watch as the live prawns are marinated in Shao Xing rice wine, then cooked in fragrant stock.

At the other end of the spectrum, salted and cured fish is a valuable source of food throughout the area, but particularly in South-east Asia. All sorts of fish and seafood are prepared in this way, either in brine or by being dried in the sun. Dried fish and shellfish also

Above: Raw prawns. Shrimps and prawns can be caught in either fresh water or the sea.

Right: Soy sauce made from fermented soya beans is one of Asia's most important contributions to the global pantry.

furnish the raw material for fish sauce and shrimp paste, essential ingredients that go under various names, and contribute a subtle but unique signature to so many dishes.

Fish sauce is not the only condiment to play a seminal role in Asian cooking. Even more important is soy sauce, fermented from soya beans, which was invented by the Chinese thousands of years ago.

Beancurd (tofu) is another soya bean product that was originally peculiar to the region, but is now widely used in the Western world, as are noodles.

Left: Dried fish can be used as a flavouring, as an ingredient in a composite dish, or as a snack food. Dried shrimps, on the other hand, have a very strong taste and are usually used as a seasoning rather than as an independent ingredient.

Right: Bok Choy tastes similar to spinach. The white stems can be cooked and eaten separately.

As well as having many ingredients in common, the countries of the Far East and South-east Asia share a similar approach to food. All prepare, cook and serve their daily meals according to the long-established principle that the Chinese call *fan-cai*. The "fan" is the main part of the meal, usually rice or another form of grain, while the "cai" includes the supplementary dishes such as fish, meat, poultry and vegetables. These elements must be balanced in every meal, as must the ingredients in every supplementary dish, so that aromas, colours, textures and tastes are all in perfect harmony.

Harmony dictates that all the dishes be served together, buffet style, rather than as separate courses. Guests begin by taking a portion of rice, and then one of the supplementary dishes on offer, relishing it on its own before taking another portion of rice and a second choice. Soup is served at the same time as other dishes, and is enjoyed throughout the meal.

Harmony extends to presentation, too, an art which reaches its apogee in Japan, where food is valued as much for its aesthetic appearance as for its flavour. In Thailand, too, food is beautifully served. Thai girls learn the art of fruit carving from a young age, and fruit (and vegetables) are cut into fabulous shapes of birds, flowers and butterflies. They are, of course, fortunate in having such wonderful raw materials. Visit the floating market in Bangkok – or, indeed, any market in this part of the world – and you will marvel at the array of vegetables and fruit on offer, many of them relatively unknown in the West until recently, when Asia became such a sought-after travel destination.

Tourism is one of the major reasons why Asian food has become so popular in Europe, America, Australia and elsewhere. Travellers discovered that Chinese food was not a single cuisine, but many, ranging from Peking cooking in the north, to the hot and spicy Sichuan-style in the west, and Cantonese in the south. Visitors to Vietnam and Thailand learned to enjoy – and distinguish between – the cuisines of those countries and, when they returned home, they wanted to be able to continue eating the meals that had been so much a part of their holiday. In major cities the world over, it is now possible to enjoy authentic Thai, Vietnamese, Indonesian, Malayan and even Filipino food, and it is only a matter of time before lesser-known cuisines are equally well represented.

Home cooks are also eager to experiment with this quick, healthy and sensual style of cooking. Ingredients such as lemon grass and galangal, which could once be bought only in oriental stores, are now readily available in many supermarkets.

There's never been a better time to discover or extend your repertoire of Asian recipes, and this book is the very best place to start.

Below: Papayas – or pawpaws as they are sometimes known – are one of the most popular tropical fruits.

CHINA AND HONG KONG

Chinese food is home cooking to at least one-quarter of the world's population, central to the

majority of people's way of life. "Have you eaten?" and "Have you taken rice?" are common

greetings throughout China. In such a vast country, there is a wealth of different styles of cooking,

and many cooks and restaurants in the West are now distinguishing between Cantonese, Sichuan

and Peking-style cooking, introducing us all to some of the world's finest food.

HOT <u>AND</u> SOUR SOUP

ONE OF CHINA'S MOST POPULAR SOUPS, THIS IS FAMED FOR ITS CLEVER BALANCE OF FLAVOURS. THE "HOT" COMES FROM PEPPER; THE "SOUR" FROM VINEGAR. SIMILAR SOUPS ARE FOUND THROUGHOUT ASIA, SOME RELYING ON CHILLIES AND LIME JUICE TO PROVIDE THE ESSENTIAL FLAVOUR CONTRAST.

SERVES 6

INGREDIENTS
  4–6 Chinese dried mushrooms
  2–3 small pieces of wood ear
    and a few golden needles (lily
    buds) (optional)
  115g/4oz pork fillet, cut into
    fine strips
  45ml/3 tbsp cornflour
  150ml/¼ pint/⅔ cup water
  15–30ml/1–2 tbsp sunflower oil
  1 small onion, finely chopped
  1.5 litres/2½ pints/6¼ cups good
    quality beef or chicken stock, or
    2 × 300g/11oz cans consommé made
    up to the full quantity with water
  150g/5oz drained fresh firm
    beancurd (tofu), diced
  60ml/4 tbsp rice vinegar
  15ml/1 tbsp light soy sauce
  1 egg, beaten
  5 ml/1 tsp sesame oil
  salt and ground white or black pepper
  2–3 spring onions, shredded,
    to garnish

1 Place the dried mushrooms in a bowl, with the pieces of wood ear and the golden needles (lily buds), if using. Add sufficient warm water to cover and leave to soak for about 30 minutes. Drain the mushrooms, reserving the soaking water. Cut off and discard the mushroom stems and slice the caps finely. Trim away any tough stem from the wood ears, then chop them finely. Using kitchen string, tie the golden needles into a bundle.

2 Lightly dust the strips of pork fillet with some of the cornflour; mix the remaining cornflour to a smooth paste with the measured water.

3 Heat the oil in a wok or saucepan and fry the onion until soft. Increase the heat and fry the pork until it changes colour. Add the stock or consommé, mushrooms, soaking water, and wood ears and golden needles, if using. Bring to the boil, then simmer for 15 minutes.

4 Discard the golden needles, lower the heat and stir in the cornflour paste to thicken. Add the beancurd, vinegar, soy sauce, and salt and pepper.

5 Bring the soup to just below boiling point, then drizzle in the beaten egg by letting it drop from a whisk (or to be authentic, the fingertips) so that it forms threads in the soup. Stir in the sesame oil and serve at once, garnished with spring onion shreds.

DRUNKEN CHICKEN

AS THE CHICKEN IS MARINATED FOR SEVERAL DAYS, IT IS IMPORTANT TO USE A VERY FRESH BIRD FROM A REPUTABLE SUPPLIER. "DRUNKEN" FOODS ARE USUALLY SERVED COLD AS PART OF AN APPETIZER, OR CUT INTO NEAT PIECES AND SERVED AS A SNACK WITH COCKTAILS.

SERVES 4–6

INGREDIENTS
    1 chicken, about 1.4kg/3lb
    1cm/½in piece of fresh root ginger,
      peeled and thinly sliced
    2 spring onions, trimmed
    1.75 litres/3 pints/7½ cups water or
      to cover
    15ml/1 tbsp salt
    300ml/½ pint/1¼ cups dry sherry
    15–30ml/1–2 tbsp brandy (optional)
    spring onions, shredded, and fresh
      herbs, to garnish

1 Rinse and dry the chicken inside and out. Place the ginger and spring onions in the body cavity. Put the chicken in a large saucepan or flameproof casserole and just cover with water. Bring to the boil, skim and cook for 15 minutes.

2 Turn off the heat, cover the pan or casserole tightly and leave the chicken in the cooking liquid for 3–4 hours, by which time it will be cooked. Drain well. Pour 300ml/½ pint/1¼ cups of the stock into a jug. Freeze the remaining stock for use in the future.

3 Remove the skin from the chicken, joint it neatly. Divide each leg into a drumstick and thigh. Make two more portions from the wings and some of the breast. Finally cut away the remainder of the breast pieces (still on the bone) and divide each breast into two even-size portions.

4 Arrange the chicken portions in a shallow dish. Rub salt into the chicken and cover with clear film. Leave in a cool place for several hours or overnight in the fridge.

VARIATION
To serve as a cocktail snack, take the meat off the bones, cut it into bite-size pieces, then spear each piece on a cocktail stick.

5 Later, lift off any fat from the stock. Mix the sherry and brandy, if using, in a jug, add the stock and pour over the chicken. Cover again and leave in the fridge to marinate for 2 or 3 days, turning occasionally.

6 When ready to serve, cut the chicken through the bone into chunky pieces and arrange on a serving platter garnished with spring onion shreds and herbs.

PEKING DUCK WITH MANDARIN PANCAKES

AS THE CHINESE DISCOVERED CENTURIES AGO, THIS IS QUITE THE BEST WAY TO EAT DUCK. THE PREPARATION IS TIME-CONSUMING, BUT IT CAN BE DONE IN EASY STAGES.

SERVES 8

INGREDIENTS

 1 duck, about 2.25kg/5¼lb
 45ml/3 tbsp clear honey
 30ml/2 tbsp water
 5ml/1 tsp salt
 1 bunch spring onions, cut into strips
 ½ cucumber, seeded and cut into
  matchsticks

For the mandarin pancakes
 275g/10oz/2½ cups strong
  white flour
 5ml/1 tsp salt
 45ml/3 tbsp peanut or sesame oil
 250ml/8fl oz/1 cup boiling water

For the dipping sauces
 120ml/4fl oz/½ cup hoisin sauce
 120ml/4fl oz/½ cup plum sauce

1 Bring a large pan of water to the boil. Place the duck on a trivet in the sink and pour the boiling water over the duck to scald and firm up the skin. Carefully lift it out on the trivet and drain thoroughly. Tie kitchen string firmly around the legs of the bird and suspend it from a butcher's hook from a shelf in the kitchen or cellar, whichever is the coolest. Place a bowl underneath to catch the drips and leave overnight.

2 Next day, blend the honey, water and salt and brush half the mixture over the duck skin. Hang up again and leave for 2–3 hours. Repeat and leave to dry completely for a further 3–4 hours.

3 Make the pancakes. Sift the flour and salt into a bowl or food processor. Add 15ml/1 tbsp of the oil, then gradually add enough of the boiling water to form a soft but not sticky dough. Knead for 2–3 minutes by hand or for 30 seconds in the food processor. Allow to rest for 30 minutes.

4 Knead the dough, then divide it into 24 pieces and roll each piece to a 15cm/6in round. Brush the surface of half the rounds with oil, then sandwich the rounds together in pairs.

5 Brush the surface of two heavy frying pans sparingly with oil. Add one pancake pair to each pan and cook gently for 2–3 minutes until cooked but not coloured. Turn over and cook for 2–3 minutes more.

6 Slide the double pancakes out of the pan and pull them apart. Stack on a plate, placing a square of non-stick baking parchment between each while cooking the remainder. Cool, wrap tightly in foil and set aside.

7 Preheat the oven to 230°C/450°F/ Gas 8. When it reaches that temperature, put the duck on a rack in a roasting tin and place it in the oven. Immediately reduce the temperature to 180°C/350°F/ Gas 4 and roast the duck for 1¾ hours without basting. Check that the skin is crisp and, if necessary, increase the oven temperature to the maximum. Roast for 15 minutes more.

8 Meanwhile, place the spring onion strips in iced water to crisp up. Drain. Pat the cucumber pieces dry on kitchen paper. Reheat the prepared pancakes by steaming the foil parcel for 5–10 minutes in a bamboo steamer over a wok or saucepan of boiling water. Pour the dipping sauces into small dishes to share between the guests.

9 Carve the duck into 4cm/1½in pieces. At the table, each guest smears some of the prepared sauce on a pancake, tops it with a small amount of crisp duck skin and meat and adds cucumber and spring onion strips before enjoying the rolled-up pancake.

COOK'S TIP

Mandarin pancakes can be cooked ahead and frozen. Simply separate the cooked pancakes with squares of freezer paper and wrap them in a plastic bag. They can be heated from frozen as described in the recipe. If time is short, use ready-made pancakes, available from large supermarkets and oriental stores.

MONGOLIAN FIREPOT

THIS MODE OF COOKING WAS INTRODUCED TO CHINA BY THE MONGOL HORDES WHO INVADED IN THE 13TH CENTURY. IT CALLS FOR PLENTY OF PARTICIPATION ON THE PART OF THE GUESTS, WHO COOK THE ASSEMBLED INGREDIENTS AT THE TABLE, DIPPING THE MEATS IN A VARIETY OF DIFFERENT SAUCES.

SERVES 6–8

INGREDIENTS
900g/2lb boned leg of lamb,
    preferably bought thinly sliced
225g/8oz lamb's liver and/or kidneys
900ml/1½ pints/3¾ cups lamb
    stock (see Cook's Tip)
900ml/1½ pints/3¾ cups
    chicken stock
1cm/½in piece fresh root ginger,
    peeled and thinly sliced
45ml/3 tbsp rice wine or
    medium-dry sherry
½ head Chinese leaves, rinsed
    and shredded
few young spinach leaves
250g/9oz fresh firm beancurd (tofu),
    diced (optional)
115g/4oz cellophane noodles
salt and ground black pepper

For the dipping sauce
50ml/2fl oz/¼ cup red wine vinegar
7.5ml/½ tbsp dark soy sauce
1cm/½in piece fresh root ginger,
    peeled and finely shredded
1 spring onion, finely shredded

To serve
steamed flower rolls
bowls of tomato sauce, sweet chilli
    sauce, mustard oil and sesame oil
dry-fried coriander seeds, crushed

COOK'S TIP
When buying the lamb, ask the butcher for the bones and make your own lamb stock. Rinse the bones and place them in a large pan with water to cover. Bring to the boil and skim the surface well. Add 1 peeled onion, 2 peeled carrots, 1cm/½in piece of peeled and bruised ginger, 5ml/1 tsp salt and ground black pepper to taste. Bring back to the boil, then simmer for about an hour until the stock is full of flavour. Strain, leave to cool, then skim and use.

1 When buying the lamb, ask your butcher to slice it thinly on a slicing machine, if possible. If you have had to buy the lamb in the piece, however, put it in the freezer for about an hour, so that it is easier to slice thinly.

2 Trim the liver and remove the skin and core from the kidneys, if using. Place them in the freezer too. If you managed to buy sliced lamb, keep it in the fridge until needed.

3 Mix both types of stock in a large pan. Add the sliced ginger and rice wine or sherry, with salt and pepper to taste. Heat to simmering point; simmer for 15 minutes.

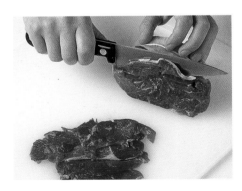

4 Slice all the meats thinly and arrange them attractively on a large platter.

5 Place the shredded Chinese leaves, spinach leaves and the diced beancurd (tofu) on a separate platter. Soak the noodles in warm or hot water, following the instructions on the packet.

6 Make the dipping sauce by mixing all the ingredients in a small bowl. The other sauces and the crushed coriander seeds should be spooned into separate small dishes and placed on a serving tray. Have ready a basket of freshly steamed flower rolls.

7 Fill the moat of the hotpot with the simmering stock. Alternatively, fill a fondue pot and place it over a burner. Each guest selects a portion of meat from the platter and cooks it in the hot stock, using chopsticks or a fondue fork. The meat is then dipped in one of the sauces and coated with the coriander seeds (if liked) before being eaten with a steamed flower roll.

8 When all or most of the meat has been eaten, top up the stock if necessary, then add the vegetables, beancurd and drained noodles. Cook for a minute or two, until the noodles are tender and the vegetables retain a little crispness. Serve the soup in warmed bowls, with any remaining steamed flower rolls.

ICED FRUIT MOUNTAIN

THIS DRAMATIC DISPLAY OF FRUIT ARRANGED ON A "MOUNTAIN" OF ICE CUBES IS BOUND TO DELIGHT YOUR GUESTS. CUT THE PIECES OF FRUIT LARGER THAN FOR A FRUIT SALAD AND SUPPLY COCKTAIL STICKS FOR SPEARING.

SERVES 6–8

INGREDIENTS
    1 star fruit
    4 kumquats
    6 physalis
    225g/8oz seedless black grapes
    225g/8oz large strawberries
    1 apple and/or 1 Asian pear
    2 large oranges, peeled
    8 fresh lychees, peeled (optional)
    1 Charentais melon and/or
      1/2 watermelon
    caster sugar, for dipping
    wedges of kaffir lime, to decorate

COOK'S TIP
The list of fruits is just a suggestion. Use any colourful seasonal fruits.

1 Slice the star fruit and halve the kumquats. Leave the hulls on the strawberries. Cut the apple and/or Asian pear into wedges, and the oranges into segments. Use a melon baller for the melon or, alternatively, cut the melon into neat wedges. Chill all the fruit.

2 Prepare the ice cube "mountain". Choose a wide, shallow bowl that, when turned upside down, will fit neatly on a serving platter. Fill the bowl with crushed ice cubes. Put it in the freezer, with the serving platter. Leave in the freezer for at least 1 hour.

3 Remove the serving platter, ice cubes and bowl from the freezer. Invert the serving platter on top of the bowl of ice, then turn platter and bowl over. Lift off the bowl and arrange the pieces of fruit on the "mountain".

4 Decorate the mountain with the kaffir lime wedges, and serve the fruit at once, handing round a bowl of sugar separately for guests with a sweet tooth.

CHINESE HONEYED APPLES

THESE SCRUMPTIOUS TREATS ARE BEST PREPARED FOR A SELECT NUMBER AS THEY REQUIRE THE COOK'S COMPLETE ATTENTION. THE HONEY COATING CRISPENS WHEN THE FRITTERS ARE DIPPED IN ICED WATER.

SERVES 4–5

INGREDIENTS
    4 crisp eating apples
    juice of 1/2 lemon
    25g/1oz/1/4 cup cornflour
    sunflower oil, for deep frying
    toasted sesame seeds,
      for sprinkling

For the fritter batter
    115g/4oz/1 cup plain flour
    generous pinch of salt
    120–150ml/4–5fl oz/1/2–2/3 cup
      water
    30ml/2 tbsp sunflower oil
    2 egg whites

For the sauce
    250ml/8fl oz/1 cup clear honey
    120ml/4fl oz/1/2 cup sunflower oil
    5ml/1 tsp white wine vinegar

1 Peel, core and cut the apples into eighths, brush each piece lightly with lemon juice then dust with cornflour. Make the sauce. Heat the honey and oil in a pan, stirring until blended. Remove from the heat and stir in the vinegar.

2 Sift the flour and salt into a bowl, then stir in the water and oil. Whisk the egg whites until stiff; fold into the batter.

3 Spear each piece of apple in turn on a skewer, dip in the batter and fry in hot oil until golden. Drain on kitchen paper, place in a dish and pour the sauce over.

4 Transfer the fritters to a lightly oiled serving dish. Sprinkle with sesame seeds. Serve at once, offering bowls of iced water for dipping.

CRISPY SHANGHAI SPRING ROLLS

IT IS SAID THAT THESE FAMOUS SNACKS WERE TRADITIONALLY SERVED WITH TEA WHEN VISITORS CAME TO CALL AFTER THE CHINESE NEW YEAR. AS THIS WAS SPRINGTIME, THEY CAME TO BE KNOWN AS SPRING ROLLS. BUY FRESH OR FROZEN SPRING ROLL WRAPPERS FROM ORIENTAL SHOPS.

MAKES 12

INGREDIENTS
12 spring roll wrappers, thawed
   if frozen
30ml/2 tbsp plain flour mixed to a
   paste with water
sunflower oil, for deep frying

For the filling
6 Chinese dried mushrooms, soaked
   for 30 minutes in warm water
150g/5oz fresh firm beancurd (tofu)
30ml/2 tbsp sunflower oil
225g/8oz finely minced pork
225g/8oz peeled cooked prawns,
   roughly chopped
2.5ml/½ tsp cornflour, mixed to a
   paste with 15ml/1 tbsp light
   soy sauce
75g/3oz each shredded bamboo shoot
   or grated carrot, sliced water
   chestnuts and bean sprouts
6 spring onions or 1 young leek,
   finely chopped
a little sesame oil

For the dipping sauce
100ml/3½ fl oz/scant ½ cup light
   soy sauce
15ml/1 tbsp chilli sauce or finely
   chopped fresh red chilli
a little sesame oil
rice vinegar, to taste

1 Make the filling. Drain the mushrooms. Cut off and discard the stems and slice the caps finely. Cut the beancurd (tofu) into slices of a similar size.

2 Heat the oil in a wok and stir-fry the pork for 2–3 minutes or until the colour changes. Add the prawns, cornflour paste and bamboo shoot or carrot. Stir in the water chestnuts.

COOK'S TIP
Thaw frozen spring roll wrappers at room temperature, open the parcel and separate with a palette knife. Cover with a damp cloth until needed.

3 Increase the heat, add the bean sprouts and spring onions or leek and toss for 1 minute. Stir in the mushrooms and beancurd. Off the heat, season, then stir in the sesame oil. Cool quickly on a large platter.

4 Separate the spring roll wrappers (see Cook's Tip). Place a wrapper on the work surface with one corner nearest you. Spoon some of the filling near the centre of the wrapper and fold the nearest corner over the filling. Smear a little of the flour paste on the free sides, turn the sides to the middle and roll up. Repeat this procedure with the remaining wrappers and filling.

5 Deep fry the spring rolls in batches in oil heated to 190°C/375°F until they are crisp and golden. Drain on kitchen paper and serve at once with the dipping sauce, made by mixing all the ingredients in a bowl.

LION'S HEAD MEAT BALLS

THESE LARGER-THAN-USUAL PORK MEAT BALLS ARE FIRST FRIED, THEN SIMMERED IN STOCK. THEY ARE TRADITIONALLY SERVED WITH A FRINGE OF GREENS SUCH AS PAK-CHOI TO REPRESENT THE LION'S MANE.

SERVES 2-3

INGREDIENTS

   450g/1lb lean pork, minced finely
     with a little fat
   4-6 drained canned water chestnuts,
     finely chopped
   5ml/1 tsp finely chopped fresh
     root ginger
   1 small onion, finely chopped
   30ml/2 tbsp dark soy sauce
   beaten egg, to bind
   30ml/2 tbsp cornflour, seasoned with
     salt and ground black pepper
   30ml/2 tbsp groundnut oil
   300ml/$\frac{1}{2}$ pint/1$\frac{1}{4}$ cups
     chicken stock
   2.5ml/$\frac{1}{2}$ tsp sugar
   115g/4oz pak-choi, stalks trimmed
     and the leaves rinsed
   salt and ground black pepper

1 Mix the pork, water chestnuts, ginger and onion with 15ml/1 tbsp of the soy sauce in a bowl. Add salt and pepper to taste, stir in enough beaten egg to bind, then form into eight or nine balls. Toss a little of the cornflour into the bowl and make a paste with the remaining cornflour and water.

VARIATION
Crab meat or prawns can be used instead of some of the pork in this recipe. Alternatively, you could try substituting minced lamb or beef for the minced pork used here.

2 Heat the oil in a large frying pan and brown the meat balls all over. Using a slotted spoon, transfer the meat balls to a wok or deep frying pan.

3 Add the stock, sugar and the remaining soy sauce to the oil that is left in the pan. Heat gently, stirring to incorporate the sediment on the bottom of the pan. Pour over the meat balls, cover and simmer for 20-25 minutes.

4 Increase the heat and add the pak-choi. Continue to cook for 2-3 minutes or until the leaves are just wilted.

5 Lift out the greens and arrange on a serving platter. Top with the meat balls and keep hot. Stir the cornflour paste into the sauce. Bring to the boil, stirring, until it thickens. Pour over the meat balls and serve at once.

TEA EGGS

THESE MARBLED EGGS WITH THEIR MAZE OF FINE LINES, HAVE AN ANTIQUE PORCELAIN APPEARANCE. TEA EGGS CAN BE SERVED AS A SNACK WITH CONGEE, A POPULAR CHINESE SOFT RICE DISH. THEY ALSO MAKE PERFECT PICNIC FARE; SHELL THEM JUST BEFORE EATING SO THAT THEY STAY MOIST.

MAKES 6

INGREDIENTS
    6 eggs
    30ml/2 tbsp dark soy sauce
    5ml/1 tsp salt
    1/2 star anise
    2 tea bags

COOK'S TIPS
• The soy sauce and tea not only colours the eggs but adds a subtle flavour as well. Use dark soy sauce, which has a stronger flavour.
• Make sure that the eggs simmer very gently and watch them carefully so that the soy sauce liquid doesn't evaporate too much. Keep topping up the liquid with recently boiled water from the kettle so that the eggs are always covered.

1 Add the eggs to a pan of cold water. Heat it to simmering point and hard boil the eggs for 20 minutes.

2 Drain the eggs and pour enough fresh cold water into the pan to cover. Set the eggs aside. When they are cold, gently roll the eggs to craze the shells without breaking them.

3 Stir the soy sauce, salt and star anise into the pan of water. Add the tea bags and eggs. Bring to the boil, cover and simmer for 1 1/2–2 hours. Top up the water to keep the eggs covered.

4 Allow the eggs to cool in the liquid overnight, then shell carefully. Quarter and serve as part of a meal.

ANITA WONG'S DUCK

THE CHINESE ARE PASSIONATELY FOND OF DUCK AND REGARD IT AS ESSENTIAL AT CELEBRATORY MEALS. TO THE CHINESE, DUCK DENOTES MARITAL HARMONY.

SERVES 4–6

INGREDIENTS
    1 duck with giblets, about
      2.25kg/5–5 1/4lb
    60ml/4 tbsp vegetable oil
    2 garlic cloves, chopped
    2.5cm/1in piece fresh root ginger,
      peeled and thinly sliced
    45ml/3 tbsp bean paste
    30ml/2 tbsp light soy sauce
    15ml/1 tbsp dark soy sauce
    15ml/1 tbsp sugar
    2.5ml/1/2 tsp five-spice powder
    3 star anise points
    450ml/3/4 pint/scant 2 cups
      duck stock (see Cook's Tip)
    salt
    shredded spring onions, to garnish

1 Make the stock (see Cook's Tip), strain into a bowl and blot with kitchen paper to remove excess fat. Measure 450ml/3/4 pint/scant 2 cups into a jug.

2 Heat the oil in a large pan. Fry the garlic without browning, then add the duck. Turn frequently until the outside is slightly brown. Transfer to a plate.

3 Add the ginger to the pan, then stir in the bean paste. Cook for 1 minute, then add both soy sauces, the sugar and the five-spice powder. Return the duck to the pan and fry until the outside is coated. Add the star anise and stock, and season to taste. Cover tightly; simmer gently for 2–2 1/2 hours or until tender. Skim off the excess fat. Leave the duck in the sauce to cool.

4 Cut the duck into serving portions and pour over the sauce. Garnish with spring onion curls and serve cold.

COOK'S TIP
To make stock, put the duck giblets in a pan with a small onion and a piece of bruised ginger. Cover with 600ml/1 pint/ 2 1/2 cups water, bring to the boil and then simmer, covered, for 20 minutes.

SICHUAN CHICKEN <u>WITH</u> KUNG PO SAUCE

THIS RECIPE, WHICH HAILS FROM THE SICHUAN REGION OF WESTERN CHINA, HAS BECOME ONE OF THE CLASSIC RECIPES IN THE CHINESE REPERTOIRE.

SERVES 3

INGREDIENTS
  2 skinless boneless chicken breasts,
    total weight about 350g/12oz
  1 egg white
  10ml/2 tsp cornflour
  2.5ml/½ tsp salt
  30ml/2 tbsp yellow salted beans
  15ml/1 tbsp hoisin sauce
  5ml/1 tsp light brown sugar
  15ml/1 tbsp rice wine or
    medium-dry sherry
  15ml/1 tbsp wine vinegar
  4 garlic cloves, crushed
  150ml/¼ pint/⅔ cup chicken stock
  45ml/3 tbsp groundnut oil or
    sunflower oil
  2–3 dried chillies, broken into
    small pieces
  115g/4oz roasted cashew nuts
  fresh coriander, to garnish

1 Cut the chicken into neat pieces. Lightly whisk the egg white in a dish, whisk in the cornflour and salt, then add the chicken and stir until coated.

COOK'S TIP
Peanuts are the classic ingredient in this dish, but cashew nuts have an even better flavour and have become popular both in home cooking and in restaurants.

2 In a separate bowl, mash the beans with a spoon. Stir in the hoisin sauce, brown sugar, rice wine or sherry, vinegar, garlic and stock.

3 Heat a wok, add the oil and then fry the chicken, turning constantly, for about 2 minutes until tender. Drain over a bowl in order to collect excess oil.

4 Heat the reserved oil and fry the chilli pieces for 1 minute. Return the chicken to the wok and pour in the bean sauce mixture. Bring to the boil and stir in the cashew nuts. Spoon into a heated serving dish and garnish with coriander leaves.

SICHUAN NOODLES <u>WITH</u> SESAME SAUCE

THIS TASTY VEGETARIAN DISH RESEMBLES THAMIN LETHOK, *A* BURMESE *DISH, WHICH ALSO CONSISTS OF FLAVOURED NOODLES SERVED WITH SEPARATE VEGETABLES THAT ARE TOSSED AT THE TABLE. THIS ILLUSTRATES NEATLY HOW RECIPES MIGRATE FROM ONE COUNTRY TO ANOTHER.*

SERVES 3–4

INGREDIENTS

   450g/1lb fresh or 225g/8oz dried
     egg noodles
   1/2 cucumber, sliced lengthways,
     seeded and diced
   4–6 spring onions
   a bunch of radishes, about 115g/4oz
   225g/8oz mooli, peeled
   115g/4oz/2 cups beansprouts, rinsed
     then left in iced water and drained
   60ml/4 tbsp groundnut oil or
     sunflower oil
   2 garlic cloves, crushed
   45ml/3 tbsp toasted sesame paste
   15ml/1 tbsp sesame oil
   15ml/1 tbsp light soy sauce
   5–10ml/1–2 tsp chilli sauce, to taste
   15ml/1 tbsp rice vinegar
   120ml/4fl oz/1/2 cup chicken stock
     or water
   5ml/1 tsp sugar, or to taste
   salt and ground black pepper
   roasted peanuts or cashew nuts,
     to garnish

1 If using fresh noodles, cook them in boiling water for 1 minute then drain well. Rinse the noodles in fresh water and drain again. Cook dried noodles according to the instructions on the packet, draining and rinsing them as for fresh noodles.

2 Sprinkle the cucumber with salt, leave for 15 minutes, rinse well, then drain and pat dry on kitchen paper. Place in a large salad bowl.

3 Cut the spring onions into fine shreds. Cut the radishes in half and slice finely. Coarsely grate the mooli using a mandolin or a food processor. Add all the vegetables to the cucumber and toss gently.

4 Heat half the oil in a wok or frying pan and stir-fry the noodles for about 1 minute. Using a slotted spoon, transfer the noodles to a large serving bowl and keep warm.

5 Add the remaining oil to the wok. When it is hot, fry the garlic to flavour the oil. Remove from the heat and stir in the sesame paste, with the sesame oil, soy and chilli sauces, vinegar and stock or water. Add a little sugar and season to taste. Warm through over a gentle heat. Do not overheat or the sauce will thicken too much. Pour the sauce over the noodles and toss well. Garnish with peanuts or cashew nuts and serve with the vegetables.

SICHUAN SPICED AUBERGINE

THIS STRAIGHTFORWARD YET VERSATILE VEGETARIAN DISH CAN BE SERVED HOT, WARM OR COLD, AS THE OCCASION DEMANDS. TOPPED WITH A SPRINKLING OF TOASTED SESAME SEEDS, IT IS EASY TO PREPARE AND TASTES ABSOLUTELY DELICIOUS.

SERVES 4–6

INGREDIENTS

2 aubergines, total weight about
    600g/1lb 6oz, cut into large chunks
15ml/1 tbsp salt
5ml/1 tsp chilli powder or to taste
75–90ml/5–6 tbsp sunflower oil
15ml/1 tbsp rice wine or
    medium-dry sherry
100ml/3½fl oz/scant ½ cup water
75ml/5 tbsp chilli bean sauce
    (see Cook's Tip)
salt and ground black pepper
a few toasted sesame seeds,
    to garnish

1 Place the aubergine chunks on a plate, sprinkle them with the salt and leave to stand for 15–20 minutes. Rinse well, drain and dry thoroughly on kitchen paper. Toss the aubergine cubes in the chilli powder.

2 Heat a wok and add the oil. When the oil is hot, add the aubergine chunks, with the rice wine or sherry. Stir constantly until the aubergine chunks start to turn a little brown. Stir in the water, cover the wok and steam for 2–3 minutes. Add the chilli bean sauce and cook for 2 minutes. Season to taste, then spoon on to a serving dish, scatter with sesame seeds and serve.

COOK'S TIP

If you can't get hold of chilli bean sauce, use 15–30ml/1–2 tbsp chilli paste mixed with 2 crushed garlic cloves, 15ml/ 1 tbsp each of dark soy sauce and rice vinegar, and 10ml/2 tsp light soy sauce.

KAN SHAO GREEN BEANS

A PARTICULAR STYLE OF COOKING FROM SICHUAN, KAN SHAO MEANS "DRY-COOKED" – IN OTHER WORDS USING NO STOCK OR WATER. THE SLIM GREEN BEANS AVAILABLE ALL THE YEAR ROUND FROM SUPERMARKETS ARE IDEAL FOR USE IN THIS QUICK AND TASTY RECIPE.

SERVES 6

INGREDIENTS

175ml/6fl oz/¾ cup sunflower oil
450/1lb fresh green beans, topped,
    tailed and cut in half
5 × 1cm/2 × ½in piece fresh
    root ginger, peeled and cut
    into matchsticks
5ml/1 tsp sugar
10ml/2 tsp light soy sauce
salt and ground black pepper

VARIATION

This simple recipe works just as well with other fresh green vegetables such as baby asparagus spears and okra.

1 Heat the oil in a wok. When the oil is just beginning to smoke, carefully add the beans and stir-fry them for 1–2 minutes until just tender.

2 Lift out the green beans on to a plate lined with kitchen paper. Using a ladle carefully remove all but 30ml/2 tbsp oil from the wok.

3 Reheat the remaining oil, add the ginger and stir-fry for a minute or two to flavour the oil.

4 Return the green beans to the wok, stir in the sugar, soy sauce and salt and pepper, and toss together quickly to ensure the beans are well coated. Serve the beans at once.

BANG BANG CHICKEN

WHAT A DESCRIPTIVE NAME THIS SPECIAL DISH FROM SICHUAN HAS! USE TOASTED SESAME PASTE TO GIVE THE SAUCE AN AUTHENTIC FLAVOUR, ALTHOUGH CRUNCHY PEANUT BUTTER CAN BE USED INSTEAD. BANG BANG CHICKEN IS PERFECT FOR PARTIES AND IDEAL FOR A BUFFET.

SERVES 4

INGREDIENTS
    3 skinless boneless chicken breasts,
      total weight about 450g/1lb
    1 garlic clove, crushed
    2.5ml/½ tsp black peppercorns
    1 small onion, halved
    1 large cucumber, peeled, seeded
      and cut into thin strips
    salt and ground black pepper

For the sauce
    45ml/3 tbsp toasted sesame paste
    15ml/1 tbsp light soy sauce
    15ml/1 tbsp wine vinegar
    2 spring onions, finely chopped
    2 garlic cloves, crushed
    5 × 1cm/2 × ½in piece fresh
      root ginger, peeled and cut
      into matchsticks
    15ml/1 tbsp Sichuan peppercorns,
      dry fried and crushed
    5ml/1 tsp light brown sugar

For the chilli oil
    60ml/4 tbsp groundnut oil
    5ml/1 tsp chilli powder

1 Place the chicken in a saucepan. Just cover with water, add the garlic, peppercorns and onion and bring to the boil. Skim the surface, stir in salt and pepper to taste, then cover the pan. Cook for 25 minutes or until the chicken is just tender. Drain, reserving the stock.

2 Make the sauce by mixing the toasted sesame paste with 45ml/3 tbsp of the chicken stock, saving the rest for soup. Add the soy sauce, vinegar, spring onions, garlic, ginger and crushed peppercorns to the sesame mixture. Stir in sugar to taste.

3 Make the chilli oil by gently heating the oil and chilli powder together until foaming. Simmer for 2 minutes, cool, then strain off the red-coloured oil and discard the sediment.

4 Spread out the cucumber batons on a platter. Cut the chicken breasts into pieces of about the same size as the cucumber strips and arrange them on top. Pour over the sauce, drizzle on the chilli oil and serve.

VARIATION
Crunchy peanut butter can be used instead of sesame paste, if preferred. Mix it with 30ml/2 tbsp sesame oil and proceed as in Step 2.

CRISPY WONTON SOUP

THE FRESHLY COOKED CRISP WONTONS ARE SUPPOSED TO SIZZLE AND "SING" IN THE HOT SOUP AS THEY ARE TAKEN TO THE TABLE.

2 Place the wonton wrappers under a slightly dampened dish towel so that they do not dry out. Next, dampen the edges of a wonton wrapper. Place about 5ml/1 tsp of the filling in the centre of the wrapper. Gather it up like a purse and twist the top or roll up as you would a baby spring roll. Fill the remaining wontons in the same way.

3 Make the soup. Drain the wood ears, trim away any rough stems, then slice thinly. Bring the stock to the boil, add the ginger and the spring onions and simmer for 3 minutes. Add the sliced wood ears, shredded spring greens, bamboo shoots and soy sauce. Simmer for 10 minutes, then stir in the sesame oil. Season to taste with salt and pepper, cover and keep hot.

SERVES 6

INGREDIENTS
2 wood ears, soaked for 30 minutes in warm water to cover
1.2 litres/2 pints/5 cups home-made chicken stock
2.5cm/1in piece fresh root ginger, peeled and grated
4 spring onions, chopped
2 rich-green inner spring greens leaves, finely shredded
50g/2oz drained canned bamboo shoots, sliced
25ml/1½ tbsp dark soy sauce
2.5ml/½ tsp sesame oil
salt and ground black pepper

For the filled wontons
5ml/1 tsp sesame oil
½ small onion, finely chopped
10 drained canned water chestnuts, finely chopped
115g/4oz finely minced pork
24 wonton wrappers
groundnut oil, for deep frying

1 Make the filled wontons. Heat the sesame oil in a small pan, add the onion, water chestnuts and pork and fry, stirring occasionally, until the meat is no longer pink. Tip into a bowl, season to taste and leave to cool.

COOK'S TIP
The wontons can be filled up to two hours ahead. Place them in a single layer on a baking sheet dusted with cornflour to prevent them from sticking and leave in a cool place.

4 Heat the oil in a wok to 190°C/375°F and fry the wontons, in batches if necessary, for 3–4 minutes or until they are crisp and golden brown all over. Ladle the soup into six warmed soup bowls and share the wontons among them. Serve immediately.

EGG FOO YUNG – CANTONESE STYLE

HEARTY AND FULL OF FLAVOUR, THIS CAN BE COOKED EITHER AS ONE LARGE OMELETTE OR AS INDIVIDUAL OMELETTES. EITHER WAY, IT IS A CLEVER WAY OF USING UP LEFTOVERS SUCH AS COOKED HAM, SEAFOOD, CHICKEN, PORK OR VEGETABLES. SERVE IT CUT INTO PIECES.

2 Beat the eggs in a bowl. Add the meat and vegetables and mix well.

3 Wipe the frying pan and heat the remaining oil. Pour in the egg mixture and tilt the pan so that it covers the base. When the omelette has set on the underside, sprinkle the top with salt, pepper and sugar.

SERVES 3–4

INGREDIENTS
    6 Chinese dried mushrooms soaked
      for 30 minutes in warm water
    50g/2oz/1 cup beansprouts
    6 drained canned water chestnuts,
      finely chopped
    50g/2oz baby spinach leaves, washed
    60ml/4 tbsp sunflower oil
    50g/2oz roast pork, cut into
      thin strips
    4 eggs
    2.5ml/½ tsp sugar
    5ml/1 tsp rice wine or
      medium-dry sherry
    salt and ground black pepper
    fresh coriander sprigs, to garnish

1 Drain the mushrooms, cut off and discard the stems; slice the caps finely and mix them with the remaining vegetables. Heat half the oil in a large heavy frying pan. Add the pork and the vegetables and toss the mixture over the heat for 1 minute.

4 Invert a plate over the pan, turn both over, and slide it back into the pan to cook on the other side. Drizzle with rice wine or sherry and serve immediately, garnished with sprigs of coriander.

CANTONESE FRIED NOODLES

CHOW MEIN IS HUGELY POPULAR WITH THE THRIFTY CHINESE WHO BELIEVE IN TURNING LEFTOVERS INTO TASTY DISHES. FOR THIS DELICIOUS DISH, BOILED NOODLES ARE FRIED TO FORM A CRISPY CRUST, WHICH IS TOPPED WITH A SAVOURY SAUCE CONTAINING WHATEVER TASTES GOOD AND NEEDS EATING UP.

SERVES 2–3

INGREDIENTS

225g/8oz lean beef steak or
   pork fillet
225g/8oz can bamboo shoots, drained
1 leek, trimmed
25g/1oz Chinese dried mushrooms,
   soaked for 30 minutes in 120ml/
   4fl oz/1/2 cup warm water
150g/5oz Chinese leaves
450g/1lb cooked egg noodles
   (255g/8oz dried), drained well
90ml/6 tbsp vegetable oil
30ml/2 tbsp dark soy sauce
15ml/1 tbsp cornflour
15ml/1 tbsp rice wine or
   medium-dry sherry
5ml/1 tsp sesame oil
5ml/1 tsp caster sugar
salt and ground black pepper

1 Slice the beef or pork, bamboo shoots and leek into matchsticks. Drain the mushrooms, reserving 90ml/6 tbsp of the soaking water. Cut off and discard the stems, then slice the caps finely. Cut the Chinese leaves into 2.5cm/1in diamond-shaped pieces and sprinkle with salt. Pat the noodles dry with kitchen paper.

2 Heat a third of the oil in a large wok or frying pan and sauté the noodles. After turning them over once, press the noodles evenly against the bottom of the pan with a wooden spatula until they form a flat, even cake. Cook over medium heat for about 4 minutes or until the noodles at the bottom have become crisp.

3 Turn the noodle cake over with a spatula or fish slice or invert on to a large plate and slide back into the wok. Cook for 3 minutes more, then slide on to a heated plate. Keep warm.

4 Heat 30ml/2 tbsp of the remaining oil in the wok. Add the strips of leek, then the meat strips and stir-fry for 10–15 seconds. Sprinkle over half the soy sauce and then add the bamboo shoots and mushrooms, with salt and pepper to taste. Toss over the heat for 1 minute, then transfer this mixture to a plate and set aside.

5 Heat the remaining oil in the wok and sauté the Chinese leaves for 1 minute. Return the meat and vegetable mixture to the wok and sauté with the leaves for 30 seconds, stirring constantly.

6 Mix the cornflour with the reserved mushroom water. Stir into the wok along with the rice wine or sherry, sesame oil, sugar and remaining soy sauce. Cook for 15 seconds to thicken. Divide the noodles among 2–3 serving dishes and pile the meat and vegetables on top.

DUCK BREASTS WITH PINEAPPLE AND GINGER

USE THE BONELESS DUCK BREASTS THAT ARE WIDELY AVAILABLE OR ALTERNATIVELY DO AS THE CHINESE AND USE A WHOLE BIRD, SAVING THE LEGS FOR ANOTHER MEAL AND USING THE CARCASS TO MAKE STOCK FOR SOUP. MUCH MORE IN LINE WITH CHINESE FRUGALITY!

SERVES 2–3

INGREDIENTS

2 boneless duck breasts
4 spring onions, chopped
15ml/1 tbsp light soy sauce
225g/8oz can pineapple rings
75ml/5 tbsp water
4 pieces drained Chinese stem ginger
   in syrup, plus 45ml/3 tbsp syrup
   from the jar
30ml/2 tbsp cornflour mixed to a
   paste with a little water
¼ each red and green pepper,
   seeded and cut into thin strips
salt and ground black pepper
cooked thin egg noodles, baby
   spinach and green beans, blanched,
   to serve

1 Strip the skin from the duck breasts. Select a shallow bowl that will fit into your steamer and that will accommodate the duck breasts side by side. Spread out the chopped spring onions in the bowl, arrange the duck breasts on top and cover with non-stick baking paper. Set the steamer over boiling water and cook the duck breasts for about 1 hour or until tender. Remove the breasts from the steamer and leave to cool slightly.

2 Cut the breasts into thin slices. Place on a plate and moisten them with a little of the cooking juices from the steaming bowl. Strain the remaining juices into a small saucepan and set aside. Cover the duck slices with the baking paper or foil and keep warm.

3 Drain the canned pineapple rings, reserving 75ml/5 tbsp of the juice. Add this to the reserved cooking juices in the pan, together with the measured water. Stir in the ginger syrup, then stir in the cornflour paste and cook, stirring until thickened. Season to taste.

4 Cut the pineapple and ginger into attractive shapes. Put the cooked noodles, baby spinach and green beans on a plate, add slices of duck and top with the pineapple, ginger and pepper strips. Pour over the sauce and serve.

SPICY SHREDDED BEEF

THE ESSENCE OF THIS RECIPE IS THAT THE BEEF IS CUT INTO VERY FINE STRIPS. THIS IS EASIER TO ACHIEVE IF THE PIECE OF BEEF IS PLACED IN THE FREEZER FOR 30 MINUTES UNTIL IT IS VERY FIRM BEFORE BEING SLICED WITH A SHARP KNIFE.

SERVES 2

INGREDIENTS
225g/8oz rump or fillet of beef
15ml/1 tbsp each light and dark
  soy sauce
15ml/1 tbsp rice wine or
  medium-dry sherry
5ml/1 tsp dark brown soft sugar or
  golden granulated sugar
90ml/6 tbsp vegetable oil
1 large onion, thinly sliced
2.5cm/1in piece fresh root ginger,
  peeled and grated
1–2 carrots, cut into matchsticks
2–3 fresh or dried chillies, halved,
  seeded (optional) and chopped
salt and ground black pepper
fresh chives, to garnish

1 With a sharp knife, slice the beef very thinly, then cut each slice into fine strips or shreds.

2 Mix together the light and dark soy sauces with the rice wine or sherry and sugar in a bowl. Add the strips of beef and stir well to ensure they are evenly coated with the marinade.

3 Heat a wok and add half the oil. When it is hot, stir-fry the onion and ginger for 3–4 minutes, then transfer to a plate. Add the carrot, stir-fry for 3–4 minutes until slightly softened, then transfer to a plate and keep warm.

4 Heat the remaining oil in the wok, then quickly add the beef, with the marinade, followed by the chillies. Cook over high heat for 2 minutes, stirring all the time.

5 Return the fried onion and ginger to the wok and stir-fry for 1 minute more. Season with salt and pepper to taste, cover and cook for 30 seconds. Spoon the meat into two warmed bowls and add the strips of carrots. Garnish with fresh chives and serve.

COOK'S TIP
Remove and discard the seeds from the chillies before you chop them – unless, of course, you like really fiery food. In which case, you could add some or all of the seeds with the chopped chillies.

STEAMED FLOWER ROLLS

THESE ATTRACTIVE LITTLE ROLLS ARE TRADITIONALLY SERVED WITH MONGOLIAN FIREPOT.

MAKES 16

INGREDIENTS
    1 quantity basic dough (below) made
      using only 5ml/1 tsp sugar
    15ml/1 tbsp sesame seed oil
    chives, to garnish

1 Divide the risen and knocked back
dough into two equal portions. Roll each
into a rectangle measuring 30 x 20cm/
12 x 8in. Brush the surface of one with
sesame oil and lay the other on top. Roll
up like a Swiss roll. Cut into 16 pieces.

COOK'S TIP
When lining the steamer, fold the paper
several times, then cut small holes like a
doily. This lets the steam circulate, yet
prevents the steamed flower rolls from
sticking to the steamer.

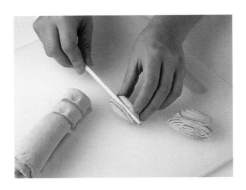

2 Take each dough roll in turn and
press down firmly on the rolled side
with a chopstick. Place the rolls on the
work surface, coiled side uppermost.

3 Pinch the opposite ends of each
roll with the fingers of both hands, then
pull the ends underneath and seal.
The dough should separate into petals.
Place the buns on non-stick baking
paper in a steamer and leave to double
in size. Steam over rapidly boiling water
for 30–35 minutes. Serve hot,
garnished with chives.

PORK-STUFFED STEAMED BUNS

*THESE TREATS ARE JUST ONE EXAMPLE OF DIM SUM, FEATHERLIGHT STEAMED BUNS WITH A RANGE OF
TASTY FILLINGS. THEY ARE NOW A POPULAR SNACK THE WORLD OVER.*

MAKES 16

INGREDIENTS
For the basic dough
    15ml/1 tbsp sugar
    about 300ml/½ pint/1¼ cups
      warm water
    25ml/1½ tbsp dried yeast
    450g/1lb/4 cups strong white flour
    5ml/1 tsp salt
    15g/½oz/1 tbsp lard
    chives, to garnish

For the filling
    30ml/2 tbsp oil
    1 garlic clove, crushed
    225g/8oz roast pork, very finely chopped
    2 spring onions, chopped
    10ml/2 tsp yellow bean
      sauce, crushed
    10ml/2 tsp sugar
    5ml/1 tsp cornflour mixed to a paste
      with water

1 Make the dough. In a small bowl,
dissolve the sugar in half the water.
Sprinkle in the yeast. Stir well, then
leave for 10–15 minutes until frothy. Sift
the flour and salt into a bowl and rub
in the lard. Stir in the yeast mixture with
enough of the remaining water to make
a soft dough. Knead on a floured
surface for 10 minutes. Transfer to an
oiled bowl and cover. Leave in a warm
place for 1 hour until doubled in bulk.

2 Meanwhile, make the filling. Heat the
oil and fry the garlic until golden, then
add the pork, spring onions, bean
sauce and sugar. Stir in the cornflour
paste and cook, stirring, until slightly
thickened. Leave to cool.

3 Knock back the dough. Knead it for
2 minutes, then divide into 16 pieces.
Roll out each piece on a floured work
surface to a 7.5–10cm/ 3–4in round.

4 Place a spoonful of filling in the
centre of each, gather up the sides and
twist the top to seal. Secure with string.

5 Set the buns on non-stick baking
paper in a large steamer and leave in a
warm place until they have doubled in
size. Steam over rapidly boiling water
for 30–35 minutes. Serve hot,
garnished with chives.

CONGEE <u>WITH</u> CHINESE SAUSAGE

CONGEE — SOFT RICE — IS COMFORT FOOD. GENTLE ON THE STOMACH, IT IS FREQUENTLY EATEN FOR BREAKFAST OR SERVED TO INVALIDS. THROUGHOUT THE EAST, PEOPLE WILL FREQUENTLY HAVE JUST A CUP OF TEA ON RISING; LATER THEY WILL SETTLE DOWN TO A BOWL OF CONGEE OR ITS REGIONAL EQUIVALENT.

SERVES 2–3

INGREDIENTS

115g/4oz/generous ½ cup long-
  grain rice
25g/1oz/3 tbsp glutinous rice
1.2 litres/2 pints/5 cups water
about 2.5ml/½ tsp salt
5ml/1 tsp sesame oil
thin slice of fresh root ginger, peeled
  and bruised
2 Chinese sausages
1 egg, lightly beaten (optional)
2.5ml/½ tsp light soy sauce
roasted peanuts, chopped, and thin
  shreds of spring onion, to garnish

1 Wash both rices thoroughly. Drain and place in a large pan. Add the water, bring to the boil and immediately reduce to the lowest heat, using a heat diffuser if you have one.

2 Cook gently for 1¼–1½ hours, stirring from time to time. If the congee thickens too much, stir in a little boiling water. It should have the consistency of creamy pouring porridge.

3 About 15 minutes before serving, add salt to taste and the sesame oil, together with the piece of ginger.

4 Steam the Chinese sausages for about 10 minutes, then slice and stir into the congee. Cook for 5 minutes.

5 Just before serving, remove the ginger and stir in the lightly beaten egg, if using. Serve hot, garnished with the peanuts and spring onions and topped with a drizzle of soy sauce.

VARIATION

If you prefer, use roast duck instead of Chinese sausages. Cut the cooked duck into bite-sized pieces and add once the rice is cooked. Congee is also popular with tea eggs.

LETTUCE PARCELS

KNOWN AS SANG CHOY *IN* HONG KONG, *THIS IS A POPULAR "ASSEMBLE-IT-YOURSELF" TREAT. THE FILLING — AN IMAGINATIVE BLEND OF TEXTURES AND FLAVOURS — IS SERVED WITH CRISP LETTUCE LEAVES, WHICH ARE USED AS WRAPPERS.*

SERVES 6

INGREDIENTS

  2 boneless chicken breasts, total
    weight about 350g/12oz
  4 Chinese dried mushrooms, soaked
    for 30 minutes in warm water
    to cover
  30ml/2 tbsp vegetable oil
  2 garlic cloves, crushed
  6 drained canned water chestnuts,
    thinly sliced
  30ml/2 tbsp light soy sauce
  5ml/1 tsp Sichuan peppercorns, dry
    fried and crushed
  4 spring onions, finely chopped
  5ml/1 tsp sesame oil
  vegetable oil, for deep frying
  50g/2oz cellophane noodles
  salt and ground black pepper
    (optional)
  1 crisp lettuce and 60ml/4 tbsp
    hoisin sauce, to serve

1 Remove the skin from the chicken breasts, pat dry and set aside. Chop the chicken into thin strips. Drain the soaked mushrooms. Cut off and discard the mushroom stems; slice the caps finely and set aside.

2 Heat the oil in a wok or large frying pan. Add the garlic, then add the chicken and stir-fry until the pieces are cooked through and no longer pink.

3 Add the sliced mushrooms, water chestnuts, soy sauce and peppercorns. Toss for 2–3 minutes, then season, if needed. Stir in half of the spring onions, then the sesame oil. Remove from the heat and set aside.

4 Heat the oil for deep frying to 190°C/ 375°F. Cut the chicken skin into strips, deep fry until very crisp and drain on kitchen paper. Add the noodles to the hot oil, deep fry until crisp. Transfer to a plate lined with kitchen paper.

5 Crush the noodles and put in a serving dish. Top with the chicken skin, chicken mixture and the remaining spring onions. Wash the lettuce leaves, pat dry and arrange on a large platter.

6 Toss the chicken and noodles to mix. Invite guests to take one or two lettuce leaves, spread the inside with hoisin sauce and add a spoonful of filling, turning in the sides of the leaves and rolling them into a parcel. The parcels are traditionally eaten in the hand.

MALAYSIA AND SINGAPORE

The food of Malaysia is a rich blend of three of the world's most exciting cuisines: Malay, Chinese and Indian. The result is the Malayan melange — a mixture of flavours, some cool, some fiery, but always in perfect harmony. Singapore promises sophistication as well as sumptuous flavours, and introduces Nonya cooking, which is famously hot and spicy.

LAKSA LEMAK

THIS SPICY SOUP IS NOT A DISH YOU CAN THROW TOGETHER IN 20 MINUTES, BUT IT IS MARVELLOUS PARTY FOOD. GUESTS SPOON NOODLES INTO WIDE SOUP BOWLS, ADD ACCOMPANIMENTS OF THEIR CHOICE, TOP UP WITH SOUP AND THEN TAKE A FEW PRAWN CRACKERS TO NIBBLE.

SERVES 6

INGREDIENTS

675g/1½lb small clams
2 × 400ml/14fl oz cans coconut milk
50g/2oz ikan bilis (dried anchovies)
900ml/1½ pints/3¾ cups water
115g/4oz shallots, finely chopped
4 garlic cloves, chopped
6 macadamia nuts or blanched
  almonds, chopped
3 lemon grass stalks, root trimmed
90ml/6 tbsp sunflower oil
1cm/½in cube shrimp paste
  (blachan)
25g/1oz/¼ cup mild curry powder
a few curry leaves
2–3 aubergines, total weight about
  675g/1¼lb, trimmed
675g/1½lb raw peeled prawns
10ml/2 tsp sugar
1 head Chinese leaves, thinly sliced
115g/4oz/2 cups beansprouts, rinsed
2 spring onions, finely chopped
50g/2oz crispy fried onions
115g/4oz fried beancurd (tofu)
675g/1½lb mixed noodles (laksa,
  mee and behoon) or one type only
prawn crackers, to serve

1 Scrub the clams and then put in a large pan with 1cm/½in water. Bring to the boil, cover and steam for 3–4 minutes until all the clams have opened. Drain. Make up the coconut milk to 1.2 litres/2 pints/5 cups with water. Put the ikan bilis (dried anchovies) in a pan and add the water. Bring to the boil and simmer for 20 minutes.

2 Meanwhile, put the shallots, garlic and nuts into a mortar. Cut off the lower 5cm/2in of two of the lemon grass stalks, chop finely and add to the mortar. Pound the mixture to a paste.

3 Heat the oil in a large heavy pan, add the shallot paste and fry until the mixture gives off a rich aroma. Bruise the remaining lemon grass stalk and add to the pan. Toss over the heat to release its flavour. Mix the shrimp paste (blachan) and curry powder to a paste with a little of the coconut milk, add to the pan and toss the mixture over the heat for 1 minute, stirring all the time, and keeping the heat low. Stir in the remaining coconut milk. Add the curry leaves and leave the mixture to simmer while you prepare the accompaniments.

4 Strain the stock into a pan. Discard the ikan bilis, bring to the boil, then add the aubergines; cook for about 10 minutes or until tender and the skins can be peeled off easily. Lift out of the stock, peel and cut into thick strips.

5 Arrange the aubergines on a serving platter. Sprinkle the prawns with sugar, add to the stock and cook for 2–4 minutes until they turn pink. Remove and place next to the aubergines. Add the Chinese leaves, beansprouts, spring onions and crispy fried onions to the platter, along with the clams.

6 Gradually stir the remaining ikan bilis stock into the pan of soup and bring to the boil. Rinse the fried beancurd in boiling water, cool slightly and squeeze to remove excess oil. Cut each piece in half and add to the soup. Lower the heat to a very gentle simmer.

7 Cook the noodles according to the instructions, drain and pile in a dish. Remove the curry leaves and lemon grass from the soup. Place the noodles, soup and the platter of seafood and vegetables on the table, along with a bowl of prawn crackers. Guests can then help themselves.

VARIATION
You could substitute mussels for clams if preferred. Scrub them thoroughly, removing any beards, and cook them in lightly salted water until they open. Like clams, discard any that remain closed.

COOK'S TIP
Dried shrimp or prawn paste, also called blachan, is sold in small blocks and is available from Asian supermarkets.

CHICKEN SATAY

ONE OF THE CLASSIC FOODS OF THE EAST. THE PIECES OF MEAT SHOULD NOT BE MORE THAN A
DELICATE MOUTHFUL OTHERWISE THEY WILL NOT ABSORB THE MARINADE SATISFACTORILY.

SERVES 4

INGREDIENTS
    4 boneless, skinless chicken breasts
    10ml/2 tsp light brown sugar

For the marinade
    5ml/1 tsp cumin seeds
    5ml/1 tsp fennel seeds
    7.5ml/1½ tsp coriander seeds
    6 shallots or small onions, chopped
    1 garlic clove, crushed
    1 lemon grass stalk, root trimmed
    3 macadamia nuts or 6 cashew nuts
    2.5ml/½ tsp ground turmeric

For the peanut sauce
    4 shallots or small onions, sliced
    2 garlic cloves, crushed
    1cm/½in cube shrimp paste
      (blachan)
    6 cashew nuts or almonds
    2 lemon grass stalks, trimmed, lower
      5cm/2in sliced
    45ml/3 tbsp sunflower oil
    5–10ml/1–2 tsp chilli powder
    400ml/14fl oz can coconut milk
    60–75ml/4–5 tbsp tamarind water or
      30ml/2 tbsp tamarind concentrate
      mixed with 45ml/3 tbsp water
    15ml/1 tbsp soft brown sugar
    175g/6oz/½ cup crunchy
      peanut butter

1 Cut the chicken into thin strips, sprinkle with the sugar and set aside.

2 Make the marinade. Dry fry the spices, then grind them to a powder. Put the shallots or onions in a mortar or a food processor and add the garlic. Roughly chop the lower 5cm/2in of the lemon grass and add it to the mortar or processor with the nuts, ground spices and turmeric. Grind to a paste and place in a bowl.

COOK'S TIP
Soaking the bamboo skewers for about 30 minutes in a large bowl of warm water before use ensures that they won't scorch when placed under the grill.

3 Add the chicken pieces and stir well until coated. Cover loosely with clear film and leave to marinate for at least 4 hours.

4 Prepare the sauce. Pound or process the shallots or onions with the garlic and shrimp paste (blachan). Add the nuts and the lower parts of the lemon grass stalks. Process to a fine purée. Heat the oil in a wok and fry the purée for 2–3 minutes. Add the chilli powder and cook for 2 minutes more.

5 Stir in the coconut milk and bring slowly to the boil. Reduce the heat and stir in the tamarind water and brown sugar. Add the peanut butter and cook over a low heat, stirring gently, until fairly thick. Keep warm. Prepare the barbecue or preheat the grill.

6 Thread the chicken on to 16 bamboo skewers. Barbecue or grill for about 5 minutes or until golden and tender, brushing with oil occasionally. Serve with the hot peanut sauce.

CHICKEN RENDANG

THIS MAKES A MARVELLOUS DISH FOR A BUFFET. SERVE IT WITH PRAWN CRACKERS OR WITH BOILED RICE AND DEEP-FRIED ANCHOVIES, ACAR BENING OR SAMBAL NANAS.

3 Add the onions, garlic and ginger to the processor. Cut off the lower 5cm/2in of the lemon grass, chop and add to the processor with the galangal. Process to a fine paste.

4 Heat the oil in a wok or large pan and fry the onion mixture for a few minutes. Reduce the heat, stir in the chilli powder and cook for 2–3 minutes, stirring constantly. Spoon in 120ml/4fl oz/½ cup of the coconut milk and add salt to taste.

5 As soon as the mixture bubbles, add the chicken pieces, turning them until they are well coated with the spices. Pour in the coconut milk, stirring constantly to prevent curdling. Bruise the top of the lemon grass stalks and add to the wok or pan. Cover and cook gently for 40–45 minutes until the chicken is tender.

SERVES 4

INGREDIENTS
    1 chicken, about 1.4kg/3lb
    5ml/1 tsp sugar
    75g/3oz/1 cup desiccated coconut
    4 small red or white onions,
       roughly chopped
    2 garlic cloves, chopped
    2.5cm/1in piece fresh root ginger,
       peeled and sliced
    1–2 lemon grass stalks, root trimmed
    2.5cm/1in piece fresh galangal,
       peeled and sliced
    75ml/5 tbsp groundnut oil or
       vegetable oil
    10–15ml/2–3 tsp chilli powder or
       to taste
    400ml/14fl oz can coconut milk
    10ml/2 tsp salt
    fresh chives and deep-fried
       anchovies, to garnish

1 Joint the chicken into 8 pieces and remove the skin, sprinkle with the sugar and leave to stand for 1 hour.

2 Dry fry the coconut in a wok or large frying pan over medium to low heat, turning all the time until it is crisp and golden. Transfer the fried coconut to a food processor and process to an oily paste. Transfer to a bowl and reserve.

6 Just before serving stir in the coconut paste. Bring to just below boiling point, then simmer for 5 minutes. Transfer to a serving bowl and garnish with fresh chives and deep-fried anchovies.

FISH MOOLIE

THIS IS A VERY POPULAR SOUTH-EAST ASIAN FISH CURRY IN A COCONUT SAUCE, WHICH IS TRULY
DELICIOUS. CHOOSE A FIRM-TEXTURED FISH SO THAT THE PIECES STAY INTACT DURING THE BRIEF
COOKING PROCESS. HALIBUT AND COD WORK EQUALLY WELL.

5 Heat the oil in a wok. Add the onion mixture and cook for a few minutes without browning. Stir in the coconut milk and bring to the boil, stirring constantly to prevent curdling.

SERVES 4

INGREDIENTS
500g/1¼lb monkfish or other firm-textured fish fillets, skinned and cut into 2.5cm/1in cubes
2.5ml/½ tsp salt
50g/2oz/⅔ cup desiccated coconut
6 shallots or small onions, roughly chopped
6 blanched almonds
2–3 garlic cloves, roughly chopped
2.5cm/1in piece fresh root ginger, peeled and sliced
2 lemon grass stalks, trimmed
10ml/2 tsp ground turmeric
45ml/3 tbsp vegetable oil
2 × 400ml/14fl oz cans coconut milk
1–3 fresh chillies, seeded and sliced
salt and ground black pepper
fresh chives, to garnish
boiled rice, to serve

1 Spread out the pieces of fish in a shallow dish and sprinkle them with the salt. Dry fry the coconut in a wok or large frying pan over medium to low heat, turning all the time until it is crisp and golden (see Cook's Tip).

2 Transfer the coconut to a food processor and process to an oily paste. Scrape into a bowl and reserve.

3 Add the shallots or onions, almonds, garlic and ginger to the food processor. Cut off the lower 5cm/2in of the lemon grass stalks, chop them roughly and add to the processor. Process the mixture to a paste.

4 Add the turmeric to the mixture in the processor and process briefly to mix. Bruise the remaining lemon grass and set the stalks aside.

6 Add the cubes of fish, most of the sliced chilli and the bruised lemon grass stalks. Cook for 3–4 minutes. Stir in the coconut paste (moistened with some of the sauce if necessary) and cook for a further 2–3 minutes only. Do not overcook the fish. Taste and adjust the seasoning.

7 Remove the lemon grass. Transfer to a hot serving dish and sprinkle with the remaining slices of chilli. Garnish with chopped and whole chives and serve with boiled rice.

COOK'S TIP
Dry frying is a feature of Malay cooking. When dry frying do not be distracted. The coconut must be constantly on the move so that it becomes crisp and of a uniform golden colour.

STEAMBOAT

THIS DISH IS NAMED AFTER THE UTENSIL IN WHICH IT IS COOKED — A TYPE OF FONDUE WITH A FUNNEL AND A MOAT. THE MOAT IS FILLED WITH STOCK, TRADITIONALLY KEPT HOT WITH CHARCOAL. ELECTRIC STEAMBOATS OR ANY TRADITIONAL FONDUE POTS CAN BE USED INSTEAD.

SERVES 8

INGREDIENTS
   8 Chinese dried mushrooms, soaked
      for 30 minutes in warm water
      to cover
   1.5 litres/2½ pints/6¼ cups well-
      flavoured chicken stock, home-made
      if possible
   10ml/2 tsp rice wine or
      medium-dry sherry
   10ml/2 tsp sesame oil
   225g/8oz each lean pork and rump
      steak, thinly sliced
   1 skinless boneless chicken breast,
      thickly sliced
   2 chicken livers, trimmed and sliced
   225g/8oz raw prawns, peeled
   450g/1lb white fish fillets, skinned
      and cubed
   200g/7oz fish balls (from Asian
      food stores)
   115g/4oz fried beancurd (tofu), each
      piece halved
   leafy green vegetables, such as
      lettuce, Chinese leaves, spinach
      leaves and watercress, cut into
      15cm/6in lengths
   225g/8oz Chinese rice vermicelli
   8 eggs
   selection of sauces, including soy
      sauce with sesame seeds; soy sauce
      with crushed ginger; chilli sauce;
      plum sauce and hot mustard
   ½ bunch spring onions, chopped
   salt and ground white pepper

1 Drain the mushrooms, reserving the soaking liquid. Cut off and discard the stems; slice the caps finely.

2 Pour the stock into a large saucepan, with the rice wine or sherry, sesame oil and reserved mushroom liquid. Bring the mixture to the boil, then season with salt and white pepper. Reduce the heat and simmer gently while you prepare the remaining ingredients.

3 Put the meat, fish, beancurd, green vegetables and mushrooms in bowls on the table. Soak the vermicelli in hot water for about 5 minutes, drain and place in eight soup bowls on a small table. Crack an egg for each diner in a small bowl; place on a side table. Put the sauces in bowls beside each diner.

4 Add the chopped spring onions to the pan of stock, bring it to a full boil and fuel the steamboat. Pour the stock into the moat and seat your guests at once. Each guest lowers a few chosen morsels into the boiling stock, using chopsticks or fondue forks, leaves them for a minute or two, then removes them with a small wire mesh ladle, a fondue fork or pair of chopsticks.

5 When all the meat, fish, beancurd and vegetables have been cooked, the stock will be concentrated and wonderfully enriched. Add a little boiling water if necessary. Bring the soup bowls containing the soaked noodles to the table, pour in the hot soup and slide a whole egg into each, stirring until it cooks and forms threads.

SIZZLING STEAK

THIS WAS ORIGINALLY A SPECIALITY OF THE COLISEUM RESTAURANT IN THE BATU ROAD IN KUALA LUMPUR. THE STEAKS WERE BROUGHT TO THE TABLE ON INDIVIDUAL HOT METAL PLATTERS, EACH SET ON A THICK WOODEN BOARD. THIS RECIPE COMES CLOSE TO RECREATING THIS WONDERFUL DISH.

SERVES 2

INGREDIENTS
   2 rump or sirloin steaks, total weight
     about 450g/1lb
   15–30ml/1–2 tbsp vegetable oil
   shredded spring onion, to garnish

For the marinade and sauce
   15ml/1 tbsp brandy
   15ml/1 tbsp rich brown sauce
   30ml/2 tbsp groundnut oil or
     sunflower oil
   a few drops of sesame oil
   2 garlic cloves, halved or crushed
   150ml/¼ pint/⅔ cup beef stock
   30ml/2 tbsp tomato ketchup
   15ml/1 tbsp oyster sauce
   15ml/1 tbsp Worcestershire sauce
   salt and sugar

1 Put the steaks side by side in a bowl. Mix the brandy, brown sauce, groundnut or sunflower oil, sesame oil and garlic in a jug and pour this marinade over the steaks. Cover loosely with clear film and leave for 1 hour, turning once. Drain the meat well, reserving the marinade.

2 Heat the oil in a heavy, ridged frying pan and fry the steaks for 3–5 minutes on each side, depending on how well done you like them. Transfer to a plate and keep warm while preparing the sauce: this allows the meat to relax, making it more tender.

3 Pour the marinade into the frying pan, if liked, discarding any large pieces of garlic.

4 Stir in the beef stock, ketchup, oyster sauce and Worcestershire sauce, with salt and sugar to taste. Bring to the boil, boil rapidly to reduce by half, then taste again for seasoning.

5 Serve each cooked steak on a very hot plate, pouring the sauce over each portion just before serving. Garnish with the shredded spring onion.

COOK'S TIP
If you don't have a ridged frying pan, simply use a large, heavy based frying pan instead.

SOTONG SAMBAL

SQUID IS READILY AVAILABLE THESE DAYS, AND IT NOW COMES CLEANED, WHICH IS A DEFINITE BONUS.
WASH THOROUGHLY INSIDE THE POCKET TO MAKE SURE THAT ALL THE QUILL HAS BEEN REMOVED.

SERVES 2

INGREDIENTS
  8 small squid, each about 10cm/4in
    long, total weight about 350g/12oz
  lime juice (optional)
  salt
  boiled rice, to serve

For the stuffing
  175g/6oz white fish fillets, such as
    sole or plaice, skinned
  2.5cm/1in piece fresh root ginger,
    peeled and finely sliced
  2 spring onions, finely chopped
  50g/2oz peeled cooked prawns,
    roughly chopped

For the sambal sauce
  4 macadamia nuts or
    blanched almonds
  1cm/1/2in piece fresh galangal,
    peeled, or 5ml/1 tsp drained
    bottled galangal
  2 lemon grass stalks, root trimmed
  1cm/1/2in cube shrimp paste
    (blachan)
  4 fresh red chillies, or to taste,
    seeded and roughly chopped
  175g/6oz small onions, roughly
    chopped
  60–90ml/4–6 tbsp vegetable oil
  400ml/14fl oz can coconut milk

1 Clean the squid, leaving them whole. Set aside with the tentacles. Put the white fish, ginger and spring onions in a mortar. Add a little salt and pound to a paste with a pestle. Use a food processor, if preferred.

2 Transfer the fish mixture to a bowl and stir in the prawns.

3 Divide the filling among the squid, using a spoon or a forcing bag fitted with a plain tube. Tuck the tentacles into the stuffing and secure the top of each squid with a cocktail stick.

4 Make the sauce. Put the macadamia nuts or almonds and galangal in a food processor. Cut off the lower 5cm/2in from the lemon grass stalks, chop them roughly and add them to the processor with the shrimp paste, chillies and onions. Process to a paste.

5 Heat the oil in a wok and fry the mixture to bring out the full flavours. Bruise the remaining lemon grass and add it to the wok with the coconut milk. Stir constantly until the sauce comes to the boil, then lower the heat and simmer the sauce for 5 minutes.

6 Arrange the squid in the sauce, and cook for 15–20 minutes. Taste and season with salt and lime juice, if liked. Serve with boiled rice.

MALAYSIAN COCONUT ICE CREAM

THIS ICE CREAM IS DELECTABLE AND VERY EASY TO MAKE IN AN ICE-CREAM MAKER, ESPECIALLY IF YOU USE THE TYPE WITH A BOWL THAT IS PLACED IN THE FREEZER TO CHILL BEFORE THE ICE-CREAM MIXTURE IS ADDED. THE ICE CREAM IS THEN CHURNED BY A MOTORIZED LID WITH A PADDLE.

2 Pour the mixture into the frozen freezer bowl of an ice-cream maker (or follow the appliance instructions) and churn till the mixture has thickened. (This will take 30–40 minutes.)

3 Transfer the mixture to a lidded plastic tub, cover and freeze until the consistency is right for scooping. If you do not have an ice-cream maker, pour the mixture into a shallow container and freeze on the coldest setting.

4 When ice crystals form around the sides of the ice cream, beat the mixture, then return it to the freezer. Do this at least twice. The more you do it, the creamier the mixture will be.

5 Make the sauce. Mix the sugar, measured water and ginger in a saucepan. Stir over medium heat until the sugar has dissolved, then bring the liquid to the boil. Add the pandan leaf, if using, tying it into a knot so that it can easily be removed with the ginger before serving. Lower the heat and simmer for 3–4 minutes. Set aside till required.

6 Serve the ice cream in coconut shells or in a bowl. Sprinkle with the strips of coconut and serve with the gula melaka sauce which can be hot, warm or cold.

SERVES 6

INGREDIENTS
    400ml/14fl oz can coconut milk
    400ml/14fl oz can condensed milk
    2.5ml/1/2 tsp salt

For the gula melaka sauce
    150g/5oz/3/4 cup palm sugar or
      muscovado sugar
    150ml/1/4 pint/2/3 cup water
    1cm/1/2in slice fresh root
      ginger, bruised
    1 pandan leaf (if available)
    coconut shells (optional) and thinly
      pared strips of coconut, to serve

1 Chill the cans of coconut and condensed milk very thoroughly. In a bowl, mix the coconut milk with the condensed milk. Gently whisk together with the salt.

COOK'S TIP
Coconut milk takes longer to freeze than double cream, so allow plenty of time for the process.

COCONUT CHIPS

COCONUT CHIPS ARE A WONDERFULLY TASTY NIBBLE TO SERVE WITH DRINKS. THE CHIPS CAN BE SLICED AHEAD OF TIME AND FROZEN (WITHOUT SALT), ON OPEN TRAYS. WHEN FROZEN, SIMPLY SHAKE INTO PLASTIC BOXES OR BAGS. YOU CAN THEN TAKE OUT AS FEW OR AS MANY AS YOU WISH FOR THE PARTY.

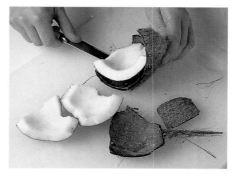

3 Having opened the coconut, use a broad-bladed knife to ease the flesh away from the hard outer shell. Taste a piece of the flesh just to make sure it is fresh. Peel away the brown skin with a potato peeler, if you like.

4 Slice the flesh into wafer-thin shavings, using a food processor, mandoline or sharp knife. Scatter these evenly all over one or two baking sheets and sprinkle with salt. Bake for about 25–30 minutes or until crisp, turning them from time to time. Cool and serve. Any leftovers can be stored in airtight containers.

COOK'S TIP

This is the kind of recipe where the slicing blade on a food processor comes into its own. It is worth preparing two or three coconuts at a time, and freezing, surplus chips. The chips can be cooked from frozen, but will need to be spread out well on the baking sheets, before being salted. Allow a little longer for frozen chips to cook.

SERVES 8 AS A SNACK

INGREDIENTS
  1 fresh coconut
  salt

1 Preheat the oven to 160°C/325°F/ Gas 3. First drain the coconut juice, either by piercing one of the coconut eyes with a sharp instrument or by breaking it carefully.

2 Lay the coconut on a board and hit the centre sharply with a hammer. The shell should break cleanly in two.

POPIAH

POPIAH ARE THE STRAITS CHINESE OR NONYA VERSION OF THE SPRING ROLL. DO NOT BE PUT OFF BY THE NUMBER OF INGREDIENTS; IT TAKES A LITTLE TIME TO GET EVERYTHING TOGETHER BUT ONCE IT IS ALL ON THE TABLE THE COOK CAN RETIRE AS GUESTS ASSEMBLE THEIR OWN.

MAKES 20–24 PANCAKES

INGREDIENTS
  40g/1½oz/⅓ cup cornflour
  215g/7½oz/generous 1¾ cups
    plain flour
  salt
  450ml/¾ pint/scant 2 cups water
  6 eggs, beaten
  lard, for frying

For the cooked filling
  30ml/2 tbsp vegetable oil
  1 onion, finely chopped
  2 garlic cloves, crushed
  115g/4oz cooked pork, chopped
  115g/4oz crab meat or peeled cooked
    prawns, thawed if frozen
  115g/4oz drained canned bamboo
    shoot, thinly sliced
  1 small yam bean, peeled and grated
    or 12 drained canned water
    chestnuts, finely chopped
  15–30ml/1–2 tbsp yellow
    salted beans
  15ml/1 tbsp light soy sauce
  ground black pepper

For the fresh fillings
  2 hard-boiled eggs, chopped
  2 Chinese sausages, steamed
    and sliced
  115g/4oz packet fried beancurd
    (tofu), each piece halved
  225g/8oz/4 cups beansprouts
  115g/4oz crab meat or peeled
    cooked prawns
  ½ cucumber, cut into matchsticks
  small bunch of spring onions,
    finely chopped
  20 lettuce leaves, rinsed and dried
  fresh coriander sprigs, to garnish
  selection of sauces, including bottled
    chopped chillies, bottled chopped
    garlic and hoisin sauce, to serve

COOK'S TIP
Yam beans are large tubers with a mild sweet texture similar to water chestnuts.

1 Sift the flours and salt into a bowl. Add the measured water and eggs and mix to a smooth batter.

2 Grease a heavy-based frying pan with lard. Heat the pan, pouring off any excess lard, then pour in just enough batter to cover the base.

3 As soon as it sets, flip and cook the other side. The pancakes should be quite thin. Repeat with the remaining batter to make 20–24 pancakes in all. Pile the cooked pancakes on top of each other, with a layer of greaseproof paper between each to prevent them sticking. Wrap in foil and keep warm in a low oven.

4 Make the cooked filling. Heat the oil in a wok and stir-fry the onion and garlic for 5 minutes until softened but not browned. Add the pork, crab meat or prawns, bamboo shoot and grated yam bean or water chestnuts. Stir-fry the mixture over a medium heat for 2–3 minutes.

5 Add the salted yellow beans and soy sauce to the wok, with pepper to taste. Cover and cook gently for 15–20 minutes, adding a little water if the mixture starts to dry out. Spoon into a serving bowl and allow to cool.

6 Meanwhile, arrange the chopped hard-boiled eggs, sliced Chinese sausages, sliced beancurd (tofu), beansprouts, crab meat or prawns, cucumber, spring onions and lettuce leaves in piles on a large platter or in separate bowls. Spoon the bottled chopped chillies, bottled chopped garlic and hoisin into small bowls.

7 Each person makes up his or her own popiah by spreading a very small amount of chopped chilli, garlic or hoisin sauce on a pancake, adding a lettuce leaf, a little of the cooked filling and a small selection of the fresh ingredients. The pancake wrapper should not be over-filled.

8 The ends can be tucked in and the pancake rolled up in typical spring roll fashion, then eaten in the hand. They also look attractive simply rolled with the filling showing. The popiah can be filled and rolled before guests arrive, in which case, garnish with sprigs of coriander. It is more fun though for everyone to fill and roll their own.

SAMOSAS

These tasty snacks are enjoyed the world over. Throughout the East, they are sold by street vendors, and eaten at any time of day. Filo pastry can be used if preferred.

MAKES ABOUT 20

INGREDIENTS

1 packet 25cm/10in square spring
  roll wrappers, thawed if frozen
30ml/2 tbsp plain flour, mixed to a
  paste with water
vegetable oil, for deep frying
coriander leaves, to garnish
cucumber, carrot and celery, cut into
  matchsticks, to serve (optional)

For the filling
25g/1oz/2 tbsp ghee or unsalted butter
1 small onion, finely chopped
1cm/1/2in piece fresh root ginger,
  peeled and chopped
1 garlic clove, crushed
2.5ml/1/2 tsp chilli powder
1 large potato, about 225g/8oz,
  cooked until just tender and finely
  diced
50g/2oz/1/2 cup cauliflower florets,
  lightly cooked, chopped into
  small pieces
50g/2oz/1/2 cup frozen peas, thawed
5–10ml/1–2 tsp garam masala
15ml/1 tbsp chopped fresh coriander
  (leaves and stems)
squeeze of lemon juice
salt

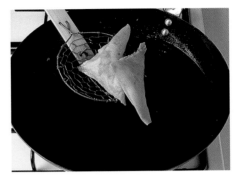

2 Cut the spring roll wrappers into three strips (or two for larger samosas). Brush the edges with a little of the flour paste. Place a small spoonful of filling about 2cm/3/4in in from the edge of one strip. Fold one corner over the filling to make a triangle and continue this folding until the entire strip has been used and a triangular pastry has been formed. Seal any open edges with more flour and water paste, if necessary adding more water if the paste is very thick.

3 Heat the oil for deep frying to 190°C/375°F and fry the samosas, a few at a time, until golden and crisp. Drain well on kitchen paper and serve hot garnished with coriander leaves and accompanied by cucumber, carrot and celery matchsticks, if liked.

COOK'S TIP
Prepare samosas in advance by frying until just cooked through and draining. Cook in hot oil for a few minutes to brown and drain again before serving.

1 Heat the ghee or butter in a large wok and fry the onion, ginger and garlic for 5 minutes until the onion has softened. Add the chilli powder, cook for 1 minute, then stir in the potato, cauliflower and peas. Sprinkle with garam masala and set aside to cool. Stir in the chopped coriander, lemon juice and salt.

CHA SHAO

THIS DISH IS OFTEN KNOWN AS BARBECUED PORK AND IS VERY POPULAR IN SOUTHERN CHINA AND MALAYSIA AS WELL AS SINGAPORE. IF YOU LIKE, THE MARINADE CAN BE HEATED THOROUGHLY, THEN SERVED WITH THE MEAT AS A SAUCE.

SERVES 6

INGREDIENTS
900g/2lb pork fillet, trimmed
15ml/1 tbsp clear honey
45ml/3 tbsp rice wine or
  medium-dry sherry
spring onion curls, to garnish

For the marinade
150ml/1/4 pint/2/3 cup dark
  soy sauce
90ml/6 tbsp rice wine or
  medium-dry sherry
150ml/1/4 pint/2/3 cup well-flavoured
  chicken stock
15ml/1 tbsp soft brown sugar
1cm/1/2in piece fresh root ginger,
  peeled and finely sliced
40ml/21/2 tbsp chopped onion

1 Mix all the marinade ingredients in a saucepan and stir over a medium heat until the mixture boils. Lower the heat and simmer gently for 15 minutes, stirring from time to time. Leave to cool.

2 Put the pork fillets in a shallow dish that is large enough to hold them side by side. Pour over 250ml/8fl oz/1 cup of the marinade, cover and chill for at least 8 hours, turning the meat over several times.

COOK'S TIP
You will have extra marinade when making this dish. Chill or freeze this and use to baste other grilled dishes or meats such as spare ribs.

3 Preheat the oven to 200°C/400°F/ Gas 6. Drain the pork fillets, reserving the marinade in the dish. Place the meat on a rack over a roasting tin and pour water into the tin to a depth of 1cm/1/2in. Place the tin in the oven and roast for 20 minutes.

4 Stir the honey and rice wine or sherry into the marinade. Remove the meat from the oven and place in the marinade, turning to coat. Put back on the rack and roast for 20–30 minutes or until cooked. Serve hot or cold, in slices, garnished with spring onion curls.

CHILLI CRABS

EAT THESE CRABS SINGAPOREAN STYLE, WITH THE FINGERS. GIVE GUESTS CRAB CRACKERS FOR THE CLAWS AND HAVE SOME FINGER BOWLS OR HOT TOWELS TO HAND AS IT WILL BE MESSY!

SERVES 4

INGREDIENTS

    2 cooked crabs, each about
      675g/1½lb
    90ml/6 tbsp sunflower oil
    2.5cm/1in piece fresh root ginger,
      peeled and chopped
    2–3 garlic cloves, crushed
    1–2 red chillies, seeded and pounded
      to a paste
    175ml/6fl oz/¾ cup tomato ketchup
    30ml/2 tbsp soft brown sugar
    15ml/1 tbsp light soy sauce
    salt
    120ml/4fl oz/½ cup boiling water
    hot toast and cucumber chunks,
      to serve

COOK'S TIP
Ready-cooked whole crabs are available
from supermarkets and fish shops.

1 To prepare the crabs twist off the large claws, then turn the crab on its back with its mouth and eyes facing away from you. Using both of your thumbs, push the body, with the small legs attached, upwards from beneath the flap, separating the body from the main shell in the process. Discard the stomach sac and grey spongy lungs known as "dead men's fingers".

2 Using a teaspoon scrape the brown creamy meat from the large shell into a small bowl. Twist the legs from the body. Cut the body section in half. Pick out the white meat. If liked, pick out the meat from the legs, or leave for guests to remove at the table.

3 Heat the oil in a wok and gently fry the ginger, garlic and fresh chilli paste for 1–2 minutes without browning. Stir in the ketchup, sugar and soy sauce, with salt to taste and heat gently.

4 Stir in the crab meat together with the claws and crab legs, if these were reserved. Pour in the boiling water, stir well and cook over a high heat until heated through. Pile the crab and crab claws mixture on serving plates with the chunks of cucumber and serve with pieces of toast.

NONYA PORK SATAY

WHEN CHINESE MERCHANTS CAME TO SINGAPORE AND PENANG AND TOOK MALAY WIVES, CULINARY TURMOIL ENSUED. THEIR BELOVED PORK WAS FORBIDDEN TO THEIR MUSLIM WIVES. NONYA, THE STYLE OF COOKING THAT EMERGED, IS A TESTAMENT TO COMPROMISE — MOSTLY BY THE WIVES.

MAKES 8–12

INGREDIENTS

    450g/1lb pork fillet
    15ml/1tbsp light brown sugar
    1cm/½in cube shrimp paste
      (blachan)
    1–2 lemon grass stalks
    30ml/2 tsp coriander seeds, dry-fried
    6 macadamia nuts or blanched
      almonds, if preferred
    2 onions, roughly chopped
    3–6 fresh red chillies, seeded and
      roughly chopped
    2.5ml/½ tsp ground turmeric
    300ml/½ pint/1¼ cups canned
      coconut milk
    30ml/2 tbsp groundnut oil or
      sunflower oil
    salt

1 Soak 8–12 bamboo skewers in water for at least an hour to prevent them from scorching when they are placed under the grill.

2 Cut the pork into small chunks, then spread it out in a single layer in a shallow dish. Sprinkle with sugar to help release the juices. Fry the shrimp paste (blachan) briefly in a foil parcel in a dry frying pan or warm it on a skewer held over the gas flame.

COOK'S TIP
Nonya Pork Satay can be served as part of a meal or as a snack, in which case serve with cubes of cucumber, which contrast well with the spicy meat.

3 Cut off the lower 5cm/2in of the lemon grass stalks and chop finely. Process the dry-fried coriander seeds to a powder in a food processor. Add the nuts and chopped lemon grass, process briefly, then add the onions, chillies, shrimp paste, turmeric and a little salt; process to a fine paste. Pour in the coconut milk and oil. Switch the machine on very briefly to mix. Pour the mixture over the pork and leave to marinate for 1–2 hours.

4 Preheat the grill or prepare the barbecue. Thread three or four pieces of marinated pork on each bamboo skewer and grill or barbecue for 8–10 minutes until tender, basting frequently with the remaining marinade. Serve at once.

SAMBAL NANAS

SAMBALS ARE THE LITTLE SIDE DISHES SERVED AT ALMOST EVERY MALAY MEAL. IN POORER SOCIETIES, A MAIN MEAL MAY SIMPLY BE A BOWL OF RICE AND A SAMBAL MADE FROM POUNDED SHRIMP PASTE, CHILLIES AND LIME JUICE. THIS SAMBAL INCLUDES CUCUMBER AND PINEAPPLE.

SERVES 8–10 AS AN ACCOMPANIMENT

INGREDIENTS
1 small or 1/2 large fresh
  ripe pineapple
1/2 cucumber, halved lengthways
50g/2oz dried shrimps
1 large fresh red chilli, seeded
1cm/1/2in cube shrimp paste
  (blachan), prepared (see Cook's Tip)
juice of 1 large lemon or lime
light brown sugar, to taste (optional)

1 Cut off both ends of the pineapple. Stand it upright on a board, then slice off the skin from top to bottom, cutting out the spines. Slice the pineapple, removing the central core. Cut into thin slices and set aside.

2 Trim the ends from the cucumber and slice thinly. Sprinkle with salt and set aside. Place the dried shrimps in a food processor and chop fairly finely. Add the chilli, prepared shrimp paste (blachan) and lemon or lime juice and process again to a paste.

3 Rinse the cucumber, drain and dry on kitchen paper. Mix with the pineapple and chill. Just before serving, spoon in the spice mixture with sugar to taste. Mix well and serve.

COOK'S TIP
The pungent shrimp paste, also called blachan, is popular in many South-east Asian countries, and is available in Asian supermarkets. Since it can taste a bit raw in a sambal, dry fry it by wrapping in foil and heating in a frying pan over a low heat for 5 minutes, turning from time to time. If the shrimp paste is to be fried with other spices, this preliminary cooking can be eliminated.

INDIAN MEE GORENG

THIS IS A TRULY INTERNATIONAL DISH COMBINING INDIAN, CHINESE AND WESTERN INGREDIENTS. IT IS A DELICIOUS TREAT FOR LUNCH OR SUPPER AND IN SINGAPORE AND MALAYSIA CAN BE BOUGHT IN MANY STREETS FROM ONE OF THE MANY HAWKERS' STALLS.

2 If using fried beancurd, cut each cube in half, refresh it in a pan of boiling water, then drain well. Heat 30ml/2 tbsp of the oil in a large frying pan. If using plain beancurd, cut into cubes and fry until brown, then lift it out with a slotted spoon and set aside.

3 Beat the eggs with the water and seasoning. Add to the oil in the frying pan and cook without stirring until set. Flip over, cook the other side, then slide it out of the pan, roll up and slice thinly.

SERVES 4–6

INGREDIENTS

   450g/1lb fresh yellow egg noodles
   60–90ml/4–6 tbsp vegetable oil
   115g/4oz fried beancurd (tofu) or
     150g/5oz firm beancurd (tofu)
   2 eggs
   30ml/2 tbsp water
   1 onion, sliced
   1 garlic clove, crushed
   15ml/1 tbsp light soy sauce
   30–45ml/2–3 tbsp tomato ketchup
   15ml/1 tbsp chilli sauce (or to taste)
   1 large cooked potato, diced
   4 spring onions, shredded
   1–2 fresh green chillies, seeded
     and finely sliced (optional)

1 Bring a large saucepan of water to the boil, add the fresh egg noodles and cook for just 2 minutes. Drain the noodles and immediately rinse them under cold water to halt cooking. Drain again and set aside.

4 Heat the remaining oil in a wok and fry the onion and garlic for 2–3 minutes. Add the drained noodles, soy sauce, ketchup and chilli sauce. Toss well over medium heat for 2 minutes, then add the diced potato. Reserve a few spring onions for garnish and stir the rest into the noodles with the chilli, if using, and the beancurd.

5 When hot, stir in the omelette. Serve on a hot platter garnished with the remaining spring onion.

THAILAND
AND BURMA

To eat a Thai meal is an exquisite experience. Curries are spicy but subtle; soups are

legendary and even the humble fish cake can be sensational if the product of an

accomplished cook. Burma has a more robust but equally interesting cuisine,

and is famous for one of the world's most delicious fish soups, Mohingha.

THAI SPRING ROLLS

CRUNCHY SPRING ROLLS ARE AS POPULAR IN THAILAND AS THEY ARE IN CHINA. THAIS FILL THEIR VERSION WITH A DELICIOUS GARLIC, PORK AND NOODLE MIXTURE.

MAKES ABOUT 24

INGREDIENTS
  24 × 15cm/6in square spring
    roll wrappers
  30ml/2 tbsp plain flour
  vegetable oil, for deep frying
  Thai sweet chilli dipping sauce, to
    serve (optional)

For the filling
  4–6 Chinese dried mushrooms,
    soaked for 30 minutes in warm
    water to cover
  50g/2oz cellophane noodles
  30ml/2 tbsp vegetable oil
  2 garlic cloves, chopped
  2 fresh red chillies, seeded
    and chopped
  225g/8oz minced pork
  50g/2oz peeled cooked prawns,
    thawed if frozen
  30ml/2 tbsp nam pla (fish sauce)
  5ml/1 tsp sugar
  1 carrot, grated
  50g/2oz drained canned bamboo
    shoots, chopped
  50g/2oz/1 cup beansprouts
  2 spring onions, finely chopped
  15ml/1 tbsp chopped fresh coriander
  ground black pepper

1 Make the filling. Drain the soaked mushrooms. Cut off the mushroom stems and discard; chop the caps finely.

2 Place the noodles in a large bowl, cover with boiling water and soak for 10 minutes. Drain the noodles and snip them into 5cm/2in lengths.

3 Heat the oil in a wok, add the garlic and chillies and stir-fry for 30 seconds. Transfer to a plate, add the pork and cook, stirring, until it has browned.

4 Add the noodles, mushrooms and prawns. Stir in the nam pla (fish sauce) and sugar, then add pepper to taste.

5 Tip the noodle mixture into a bowl and stir in the carrot, bamboo shoots, beansprouts, spring onions and chopped coriander together with the reserved chilli mixture.

6 Unwrap the spring roll wrappers. Cover them with a dampened dish towel while you are making the rolls, so that they do not dry out. Put the flour in a small bowl and stir in a little water to make a paste. Place a spoonful of filling in the centre of a spring roll wrapper.

7 Turn the bottom edge over to cover the filling, then fold in the left and right sides. Roll the wrapper up almost to the top then brush the top edge with the flour paste and seal. Fill the remaining wrappers in the same way.

8 Heat the oil in a wok or deep-fryer. Fry the spring rolls, a few at a time, until crisp and golden brown. Drain on kitchen paper and keep hot while cooking successive batches. Serve hot with Thai sweet chilli sauce, if you like.

COOK'S TIP
Fish sauce (nam pla) is made from anchovies, which are salted, then fermented in wooden barrels. The sauce accentuates the flavour of food, and does not necessarily impart a fishy flavour.

CRISP-FRIED CRAB CLAWS

CRAB CLAWS ARE READILY AVAILABLE IN THE FREEZER CABINET IN MANY ORIENTAL STORES AND SUPERMARKETS. THAW OUT THOROUGHLY AND DRY ON KITCHEN PAPER BEFORE DIPPING IN THE BATTER.

SERVES 4

INGREDIENTS
    50g/2oz/⅓ cup rice flour
    15ml/1 tbsp cornflour
    2.5ml/½ tsp sugar
    1 egg
    60ml/4 tbsp cold water
    1 lemon grass stalk, root trimmed
    2 garlic cloves, finely chopped
    15ml/1 tbsp chopped fresh coriander
    1–2 fresh red chillies, seeded and
      finely chopped
    5ml/1 tsp nam pla (fish sauce)
    vegetable oil, for frying
    12 half-shelled crab claws
    ground black pepper

For the chilli vinegar dip
    45ml/3 tbsp sugar
    120ml/4fl oz/½ cup water
    120ml/4fl oz/½ cup red wine vinegar
    15ml/1 tbsp nam pla (fish sauce)
    2–4 fresh red chillies, seeded
      and chopped

1 Make the chilli dip. Mix the sugar and water in a saucepan, stirring until the sugar has dissolved then bring to the boil. Lower the heat and simmer for 5–7 minutes. Stir in the rest of the ingredients and set aside.

2 Combine the rice flour, cornflour and sugar in a bowl. Beat the egg with the cold water, then stir the egg and water mixture into the flour mixture and mix well until it forms a light batter.

3 Cut off the lower 5cm/2in of the lemon grass stalk and chop it finely. Add the lemon grass to the batter, with the garlic, coriander, red chillies and nam pla (fish sauce). Stir in pepper to taste.

4 Heat the oil in a wok or deep-fryer. Pat the crab claws dry and dip into the batter. Drop the battered claws into the hot oil, a few at a time. Fry until golden brown. Drain on kitchen paper and keep hot. Pour the dip into a serving bowl and serve with the crab claws.

FISH CAKES WITH CUCUMBER RELISH

THESE WONDERFUL SMALL FISH CAKES ARE A VERY FAMILIAR AND POPULAR APPETIZER IN THAILAND
AND INCREASINGLY THROUGHOUT SOUTH-EAST ASIA. THEY ARE USUALLY SERVED WITH THAI BEER.

MAKES ABOUT 12

INGREDIENTS
5 kaffir lime leaves
300g/11oz cod, cut into chunks
30ml/2 tbsp red curry paste
1 egg
30ml/2 tbsp nam pla (fish sauce)
5ml/1 tsp sugar
30ml/2 tbsp cornflour
15ml/1 tbsp chopped fresh coriander
50g/2oz green beans, finely sliced
vegetable oil, for frying
fresh Chinese mustard cress or
   coriander leaves, to garnish

For the cucumber relish
60ml/4 tbsp coconut or rice vinegar
50g/2oz/¼ cup sugar
1 head pickled garlic
15ml/1 tbsp fresh root ginger
1 cucumber, cut into matchsticks
4 shallots, finely sliced

1 Make the cucumber relish. Bring the vinegar and sugar to the boil in a small pan with 60ml/4 tbsp water, stirring until the sugar has dissolved. Remove from the heat and cool.

2 Separate the pickled garlic into cloves. Chop these finely along with the ginger and place in a bowl. Add the cucumber and shallots, pour over the vinegar mixture and mix lightly.

3 Reserve two kaffir lime leaves for garnish and thinly slice the remainder. Put the chunks of fish, curry paste and egg in a food processor and process to a smooth paste. Transfer the mixture to a bowl and stir in the nam pla (fish sauce), sugar, cornflour, sliced kaffir lime leaves, coriander and green beans. Mix well, then shape the mixture into about twelve 5mm/¼in thick cakes, measuring about 5cm/2in in diameter.

4 Heat the oil in a wok or deep-frying pan. Fry the fish cakes, a few at a time, for about 4–5 minutes until cooked and evenly brown.

5 Lift out the fish cakes and drain them on kitchen paper. Keep each batch hot while frying successive batches. Garnish with the reserved kaffir leaves and serve with the cucumber relish.

GINGER, CHICKEN <u>AND</u> COCONUT SOUP

THIS AROMATIC SOUP IS RICH WITH COCONUT MILK AND INTENSELY FLAVOURED WITH GALANGAL, LEMON GRASS AND KAFFIR LIME LEAVES.

SERVES 4–6

INGREDIENTS
    4 lemon grass stalks, roots trimmed
    2 × 400ml/14fl oz cans coconut milk
    475ml/16fl oz/2 cups chicken stock
    2.5cm/1in piece galangal, peeled and
      thinly sliced
    10 black peppercorns, crushed
    10 kaffir lime leaves, torn
    300g/11oz skinless boneless chicken
      breasts, cut into thin strips
    115g/4oz/1 cup button mushrooms
    50g/2oz/1/2 cup baby corn cobs,
      quartered lengthways
    60ml/4 tbsp lime juice
    45ml/3 tbsp nam pla (fish sauce)
    chopped fresh red chillies, spring
      onions and fresh coriander leaves,
      to garnish

1 Cut off the lower 5cm/2in from each lemon grass stalk and chop it finely. Bruise the remaining pieces of stalk. Bring the coconut milk and chicken stock to the boil in a large pan. Add all the lemon grass, the galangal, peppercorns and half the lime leaves, lower the heat and simmer gently for 10 minutes. Strain into a clean pan.

2 Return the soup to the heat, then add the chicken, mushrooms and corn. Simmer for 5–7 minutes or until the chicken is cooked.

3 Stir in the lime juice and nam pla (fish sauce), then add the remaining lime leaves. Serve hot, garnished with chillies, spring onions and coriander.

HOT-AND-SOUR PRAWN SOUP

THIS IS A CLASSIC THAI SEAFOOD SOUP – TOM YAM KUNG – AND IT IS PROBABLY THE MOST POPULAR AND WELL-KNOWN SOUP FROM THAT COUNTRY.

SERVES 4–6

INGREDIENTS
    450g/1lb raw king prawns, thawed
      if frozen
    1 litre/1¾ pints/4 cups chicken
      stock or water
    3 lemon grass stalks, root trimmed
    10 kaffir lime leaves, torn in half
    225g/8oz can straw mushrooms
    45ml/3 tbsp nam pla (fish sauce)
    60ml/4 tbsp lime juice
    30ml/2 tbsp chopped spring onion
    15ml/1 tbsp fresh coriander leaves
    4 fresh red chillies, seeded
      and thinly sliced
    salt and ground black pepper

1 Shell the prawns, putting the shells in a colander. Devein the prawns and set them aside.

2 Rinse the shells under cold water, then put in a large saucepan with the stock or water. Bring to the boil.

3 Bruise the lemon grass stalks and add them to the stock with half the lime leaves. Simmer gently for 5–6 minutes, until the stock is fragrant.

4 Strain the stock, return it to the clean pan and reheat. Add the drained mushrooms and the prawns, then cook until the prawns turn pink.

5 Stir in the nam pla (fish sauce), lime juice, spring onion, coriander, chillies and the remaining lime leaves. Taste and adjust the seasoning. The soup should be sour, salty, spicy and hot.

STIR-FRIED CHICKEN WITH BASIL AND CHILLI

THIS QUICK AND EASY CHICKEN DISH IS AN EXCELLENT INTRODUCTION TO THAI CUISINE. THAI BASIL, WHICH IS SOMETIMES KNOWN AS HOLY BASIL, HAS A UNIQUE, PUNGENT FLAVOUR THAT IS BOTH SPICY AND SHARP. DEEP FRYING THE LEAVES ADDS ANOTHER DIMENSION TO THIS DISH.

SERVES 4–6

INGREDIENTS

45ml/3 tbsp vegetable oil
4 garlic cloves, thinly sliced
2–4 fresh red chillies, seeded
 and finely chopped
450g/1lb skinless boneless chicken
 breasts, cut into bite-size pieces
45ml/3 tbsp nam pla (fish sauce)
10ml/2 tsp dark soy sauce
5ml/1 tsp sugar
10–12 Thai basil leaves
2 fresh red chillies, seeded and
 finely chopped and about 20 deep-
 fried Thai basil leaves, to garnish

1 Heat the oil in a wok or large frying pan. Add the garlic and chillies and stir-fry over a medium heat for 1–2 minutes until the garlic is golden.

2 Add the pieces of chicken to the wok or pan and stir-fry until the chicken changes colour.

3 Stir in the nam pla (fish sauce), soy sauce and sugar. Continue to stir-fry the mixture for 3–4 minutes or until the chicken is fully cooked with the sauce.

4 Stir in the fresh Thai basil leaves. Spoon the entire mixture on to a warm serving platter, or individual serving dishes and garnish with the sliced chillies and deep-fried Thai basil.

COOK'S TIP

To deep fry Thai basil leaves, first make sure that the leaves are completely dry or they will splutter when added to the oil. Deep fry the leaves briefly in hot oil until they are crisp and transluscent – this will only take about 30–40 seconds. Lift out the leaves using a slotted spoon or wire basket and leave them to drain on kitchen paper.

GREEN PAPAYA SALAD

THIS SALAD APPEARS IN MANY GUISES IN SOUTH-EAST ASIA. AS GREEN PAPAYA IS NOT EASY TO GET HOLD OF, FINELY GRATED CARROTS, CUCUMBER OR GREEN APPLE CAN BE USED INSTEAD. ALTERNATIVELY, USE VERY THINLY SLICED WHITE CABBAGE.

2 Put the garlic, shallots, chillies and salt in a large mortar and grind to a paste with a pestle. Add the shredded papaya, a little at a time, pounding until it becomes slightly limp and soft.

3 Add the sliced beans and wedges of tomato to the mortar and crush them lightly with the pestle.

SERVES 4

INGREDIENTS
- 1 green papaya
- 4 garlic cloves, roughly chopped
- 15ml/1 tbsp chopped shallots
- 3–4 fresh red chillies, seeded and sliced
- 2.5ml/½ tsp salt
- 2–3 snake beans or 6 green beans, cut into 2cm/¾in lengths
- 2 tomatoes, cut into thin wedges
- 45ml/3 tbsp nam pla (fish sauce)
- 15ml/1 tbsp caster sugar
- juice of 1 lime
- 30ml/2 tbsp crushed roasted peanuts
- sliced fresh red chillies, to garnish

1 Cut the papaya in half lengthways. Scrape out the seeds with a spoon, then peel using a swivel vegetable peeler or a small sharp knife. Shred the flesh finely using a food processor or grater.

4 Season the mixture with the nam pla (fish sauce), sugar and lime juice. Transfer the salad to a serving dish and sprinkle with crushed peanuts and garnish with sliced red chillies.

STUFFED THAI OMELETTES

INDIVIDUAL OMELETTES CAN BE MADE OR MAKE TWO LARGE OMELETTE PARCELS TO SERVE FOUR. THEY ARE REMARKABLY EASY TO MAKE AND MAKE A TASTY LUNCH OR LIGHT SUPPER.

2 Stir in the **nam pla** (fish sauce), sugar and tomatoes, with pepper to taste. Simmer for 5–8 minutes, until the sauce thickens. Remove from the heat and stir in the chopped fresh coriander.

3 Make the omelettes. Whisk the eggs and nam pla in a bowl. Heat a little of the oil in a 20cm/8in omelette pan. Add a quarter or half of the egg mixture, depending on whether you wish to make individual parcels or cut them in half. Tilt the pan to spread the egg into a thin, even sheet. As soon as it sets, spoon some of the filling over the centre of the omelette. Fold the top and bottom over, then the right and left sides to make a neat, square parcel.

4 Slide the omelette out on to a warm serving dish, folded side down, and keep hot while you make the remaining omelette(s). Serve garnished with sprigs of coriander.

SERVES 3–4

INGREDIENTS
    30ml/2 tbsp vegetable oil
    2 garlic cloves, finely chopped
    1 small onion, finely chopped
    225g/8oz minced pork
    30ml/2 tbsp nam pla (fish sauce)
    5ml/1 tsp sugar
    2 tomatoes, peeled and chopped
    15ml/1 tbsp chopped fresh coriander
    ground black pepper
    fresh coriander sprigs, to garnish

For the omelettes
    6 eggs
    15ml/1 tbsp nam pla (fish sauce)
    about 30ml/2 tbsp vegetable oil

1 Heat the oil in a wok or frying pan. Add the chopped garlic and onion and fry for 3–4 minutes until the onion is softened. Add the minced pork and stir-fry for 7–10 minutes, until broken up and lightly browned.

VARIATION
Replace half the minced pork with peeled tiger prawns or white crab meat.

BARBECUED CHICKEN

BARBECUED CHICKEN IS SERVED ALMOST EVERYWHERE IN THAILAND, FROM PORTABLE ROADSIDE STALLS TO SPORTS STADIUMS AND EVEN ON THE BEACH.

SERVES 4–6

INGREDIENTS
    1 chicken, about 1.5kg/3–3½ lb,
      cut into 8–10 pieces
      lime wedges and fresh red chillies,
      to garnish

For the marinade
    2 lemon grass stalks, root trimmed
    2.5cm/1in piece fresh root ginger,
      peeled and thinly sliced
    6 garlic cloves, roughly chopped
    4 shallots, roughly chopped
    ½ bunch coriander roots, chopped
    15ml/1 tbsp palm sugar
    120ml/4fl oz/½ cup coconut milk
    30ml/2 tbsp nam pla (fish sauce)
    30ml/2 tbsp light soy sauce

1 First make the marinade. Cut off the lower 5cm/2in of both of the lemon grass stalks and chop them roughly. Put into a food processor along with all the other marinade ingredients and process until the mixture has reached a smooth consistency.

2 Place the chicken pieces in a dish, pour over the marinade and stir to mix well. Cover the dish and leave in a cool place to marinate for at least 4 hours or overnight.

3 Prepare the barbecue or preheat the oven to 200°C/400°F/Gas 6. If cooking in the oven, arrange the chicken pieces on a rack over a roasting tin.

4 Barbecue or bake in the oven for 20–30 minutes or until the pieces are cooked and golden brown. Turn the pieces and brush with the marinade once or twice during cooking. Transfer the chicken pieces to a serving platter and garnish with lime wedges and red chillies.

COOK'S TIP
Coconut milk is available fresh or in cans or cartons from most supermarkets, or use 50g/2oz creamed coconut, available in packets, and dissolve in warm water.

RED CHICKEN CURRY WITH BAMBOO SHOOTS

BAMBOO SHOOTS HAVE A LOVELY CRUNCHY TEXTURE. IT IS QUITE ACCEPTABLE TO USE CANNED ONES, AS FRESH BAMBOO IS NOT READILY AVAILABLE IN THE WEST. BUY CANNED WHOLE BAMBOO SHOOTS, WHICH ARE CRISPER AND OF BETTER QUALITY THAN SLICED SHOOTS. RINSE BEFORE USING.

SERVES 4–6

INGREDIENTS

1 litre/1¾ pints/4 cups coconut milk
450g/1lb skinless, boneless chicken
   breasts, cut into bite-size pieces
30ml/2 tbsp nam pla (fish sauce)
15ml/1 tbsp sugar
225g/8oz drained canned bamboo
   shoots, rinsed and sliced
5 kaffir lime leaves, torn
salt and ground black pepper
chopped fresh red chillies and kaffir
   lime leaves, to garnish

For the red curry paste
5ml/1 tsp coriander seeds
2.5ml/½ tsp cumin seeds
12–15 fresh red chillies, seeded and
   roughly chopped
4 shallots, thinly sliced
2 garlic cloves, chopped
15ml/1 tbsp chopped galangal
2 lemon grass stalks, chopped
3 kaffir lime leaves, chopped
4 fresh coriander roots
10 black peppercorns
good pinch of ground cinnamon
5ml/1 tsp ground turmeric
2.5ml/½ tsp shrimp paste (blachan)
5ml/1 tsp salt
30ml/2 tbsp vegetable oil

1 Make the curry paste. Dry fry the coriander and cumin seeds for 1–2 minutes, then put in a mortar or food processor with the remaining ingredients except the oil and pound or process to a paste.

2 Add the oil, a little at a time, mixing or processing well after each addition. Transfer to a jar and keep in the fridge until ready to use.

3 Pour half of the coconut milk into a large heavy-based saucepan. Bring the milk to the boil, stirring constantly until it has separated.

4 Stir in 30ml/2 tbsp of the red curry paste and cook the mixture for 2–3 minutes, stirring constantly. Remaining red curry paste can be kept in the fridge for up to 3 months.

5 Add the chicken pieces, nam pla (fish sauce) and sugar to the pan. Stir well, then cook for 5–6 minutes until the chicken changes colour and is cooked through, stirring constantly to prevent the mixture from sticking to the bottom of the pan.

6 Pour the remaining coconut milk into the pan, then add the sliced bamboo shoots and torn kaffir lime leaves. Bring back to the boil over a medium heat, stirring constantly to prevent the mixture sticking, then taste and add salt and pepper if necessary.

7 To serve, spoon the curry into a warmed serving dish and garnish with chopped chillies and kaffir lime leaves.

VARIATION
Instead of, or as well as, bamboo shoots, use straw mushrooms. These are available in cans from Asian stores and supermarkets. Drain well and then stir into the curry at the end of the recipe.

COOK'S TIP
It is essential to use chicken breasts, rather than any other cut, for this curry, as it is cooked very quickly. Look out for diced chicken or strips of chicken (which are often labelled "stir-fry chicken") in the supermarket.

MUSSAMAN CURRY

THIS DISH IS TRADITIONALLY MADE WITH BEEF, BUT CHICKEN, LAMB OR BEANCURD CAN BE USED. IT HAS A RICH, SWEET AND SPICY FLAVOUR AND IS BEST SERVED WITH BOILED RICE. MUSSAMAN CURRY PASTE IS AVAILABLE FROM SPECIALIST STORES OR MAKE YOUR OWN.

SERVES 4–6

INGREDIENTS
  600ml/1 pint/2½ cups canned
    coconut milk
  675g/1½ lb stewing steak, cut into
    2.5cm/1in chunks
  250ml/8fl oz/1 cup coconut cream
  45ml/3 tbsp Mussaman curry paste
    (see Cook's Tip)
  30ml/2 tbsp nam pla (fish sauce)
  15ml/1 tbsp palm sugar
  60ml/4 tbsp tamarind juice
  6 green cardamom pods
  1 cinnamon stick
  1 large potato, about 225g/8oz, cut
    into even-size chunks
  1 onion, cut into wedges
  50g/2oz/½ cup roasted peanuts

1 Bring the coconut milk to a gentle boil in a large saucepan. Add the beef, lower the heat and simmer for about 40 minutes until tender.

2 Put the coconut cream into a pan and cook for 5–8 minutes, stirring, until it separates. Stir in the Mussaman curry paste and cook rapidly until fragrant. Add to the cooked beef, and mix well.

3 Stir in the nam pla (fish sauce), sugar, tamarind juice, cardamom pods, cinnamon, potato and onion. Simmer for 15–20 minutes or until the potato is cooked. Add the peanuts and mix well. Cook for 5 minutes and serve.

COOK'S TIP
To make Mussaman curry paste, soak 12 large, seeded dried chillies, in hot water for 15 minutes. Chop finely and pound or process with 60ml/4 tbsp shallots, 5 garlic cloves, 1 lemon grass stalk base and 30ml/2 tbsp chopped galangal. Put 5ml/1 tsp cumin seeds, 15ml/1 tbsp coriander seeds, 2 cloves and 6 black peppercorns in a pan; dry fry over a low heat for 1–2 minutes. Grind to a powder; add 5ml/1 tsp shrimp paste (blachan), 5ml/1 tsp salt, 5ml/1 tsp sugar and 30ml/2 tbsp vegetable oil. Stir in the shallot mixture to make a paste.

CURRIED PRAWNS IN COCONUT MILK

ANOTHER WONDERFULLY QUICK AND EASY DISH, THIS FEATURES PRAWNS IN A SPICY COCONUT GRAVY.

SERVES 4–6

INGREDIENTS

  600ml/1 pint/2½ cups coconut milk
  30ml/2 tbsp yellow curry paste (see
    Cook's Tip)
  15ml/1 tbsp nam pla (fish sauce)
  2.5ml/½ tsp salt
  5ml/1 tsp sugar
  450g/1lb raw king prawns peeled,
    thawed if frozen
  225g/8oz cherry tomatoes
  fresh yellow and orange peppers,
    seeded and cut into thin strips,
    chives and juice of ½ lime, to
    garnish

VARIATION
Use cooked prawns for a quick version
of this dish. Add them after the tomatoes
and heat through for a minute or two.

1 Put half the coconut milk in a wok or
saucepan and bring to the boil. Add the
yellow curry paste, stir until it disperses,
then lower the heat and simmer for
about 10 minutes.

2 Add the nam pla (fish sauce), salt,
sugar and remaining coconut milk to
the sauce. Simmer for 5 minutes more.

3 Add the prawns and cherry tomatoes.
Simmer very gently for about 5 minutes
until the prawns are pink and tender.

4 Spoon into a serving dish, sprinkle
with lime juice and garnish with strips
of yellow peppers and chives.

COOK'S TIP
To make yellow curry paste, put into a
food processor or blender 6–8 fresh
yellow chillies, the chopped base of
1 lemon grass stalk, 4 chopped shallots,
4 chopped garlic cloves, 15ml/1 tbsp
chopped peeled fresh root ginger, 5ml/
1 tsp coriander seeds, 5ml/1 tsp mustard
powder, 5ml/1 tsp salt, 2.5ml/½ tsp
ground cinnamon, 15ml/1 tbsp light
brown sugar and 30ml/2 tbsp sunflower
oil. Process to a paste, scrape into a
glass jar, cover and keep in the fridge.

STEWED PUMPKIN IN COCONUT CREAM

STEWED FRUIT IS A POPULAR DESSERT IN THAILAND. PUMPKINS, BANANAS AND MELONS CAN ALL BE PREPARED IN THIS WAY, AND YOU CAN EVEN STEW SWEETCORN KERNELS OR PULSES SUCH AS MUNG BEANS AND BLACK BEANS IN COCONUT MILK.

SERVES 4–6

INGREDIENTS
   1kg/2¼lb kabocha pumpkin
   750ml/1¼ pints/3 cups
      coconut milk
   175g/6oz/¾ cup sugar
   pinch of salt
   toasted pumpkin seed kernels and
      fresh mint sprigs, to decorate

COOK'S TIP
To make the garnish, wash the pumpkin seeds to remove any fibres and pat them dry on kitchen paper. Roast them in a dry frying pan or, alternatively, spread the seeds out on a baking sheet and grill until golden brown; toss them frequently.

1 Cut the pumpkin in half using a large, sharp knife, then cut away and discard the skin. Scoop out the seed cluster and reserve a few seeds. Using a sharp knife, cut the pumpkin flesh into pieces that are about 5cm/2in long and 2cm/¾in thick.

2 In a saucepan, bring the coconut milk, sugar and salt to the boil. Add the pumpkin and simmer for about 10–15 minutes until it is tender. Serve warm, in individual dishes. Decorate each serving with a mint sprig and a few toasted pumpkin seed kernels.

MANGOES WITH STICKY RICE

EVERYONE'S FAVOURITE DESSERT: MANGOES, WITH THEIR DELICATE FRAGRANCE, SWEET AND SOUR FLAVOUR AND VELVETY FLESH, BLEND ESPECIALLY WELL WITH COCONUT STICKY RICE. YOU NEED TO START PREPARING THIS DISH THE DAY BEFORE YOU INTEND TO SERVE IT.

SERVES 4

INGREDIENTS
   115g/4oz/⅔ cup white
      glutinous rice
   175ml/6fl oz/¾ cup thick
      coconut milk
   45ml/3 tbsp sugar
   pinch of salt
   2 ripe mangoes, peeled and sliced
   strips of lime rind, to decorate

1 Rinse the glutinous rice thoroughly in several changes of cold water, then leave to soak overnight in a bowl of fresh cold water.

COOK'S TIP
Like cream, the thickest and richest part of coconut milk rises to the top. Spoon it off and pour over before serving.

2 Drain the rice and spread evenly in a steamer lined with cheesecloth. Cover and steam over simmering water for 20 minutes or until tender.

3 Reserve 45ml/3 tbsp of the top of the coconut milk. Bring the rest to the boil in a pan with the sugar and salt, stirring until the sugar dissolves. Pour into a bowl to cool.

4 Tip the cooked rice into a bowl and pour over the cooled coconut milk mixture. Stir well, then leave to stand for about 10–15 minutes.

5 Spoon the rice on to individual serving plates. Arrange mango slices on one side and then drizzle with the reserved coconut milk. Decorate with strips of lime rind and serve.

MOHINGHA

*BURMESE HOUSEWIVES BUY THIS WELL-KNOWN AND DELICIOUS ONE-COURSE MEAL FROM HAWKERS,
RECOGNIZED BY A BAMBOO POLE CARRIED ACROSS THEIR SHOULDERS. AT ONE END IS A CONTAINER
WITH A CHARCOAL FIRE AND AT THE OTHER END IS EVERYTHING ELSE THEY NEED TO MAKE THE MEAL.*

SERVES 8

INGREDIENTS
  675g/1½lb huss, cod or mackerel,
    cleaned but left on the bone
  3 lemon grass stalks
  2.5cm/1in piece fresh root
    ginger, peeled
  30ml/2 tbsp fish sauce
  3 onions, roughly chopped
  4 garlic cloves, roughly chopped
  2–3 fresh red chillies, seeded
    and chopped
  5ml/1 tsp ground turmeric
  75ml/5 tbsp groundnut oil, for frying
  400ml/14fl oz can coconut milk
  25g/1oz/3 tbsp rice flour
  25g/1oz/3 tbsp chick-pea
    flour (besan)
  pieces of banana trunk, or heart, if
    available, or 540g/1lb 5oz drained
    canned bamboo shoot, sliced
  salt and ground black pepper
  wedges of hard-boiled egg, thinly
    sliced red onions, finely chopped
    spring onions, a few deep fried
    prawns and fried chillies (see Cook's
    Tip), to garnish
  450g/1lb dried or fresh rice noodles,
    cooked according to the instructions
    on the packet, to serve

1 Place the fish in a large pan and pour in cold water to cover. Bruise two lemon grass stalks and half the ginger and add to the pan. Bring to the boil, add the fish sauce and cook for 10 minutes. Lift out the fish and allow to cool while straining the stock into a large bowl. Discard any skin and bones from the fish and break the flesh into small pieces.

COOK'S TIP
To make fried chillies, dry roast 8–10 dried red chillies in a heavy frying pan, then pound them, fry in 30ml/2 tbsp peanut oil and stir in 25g/1oz dried shrimps (pounded).

2 Cut off the lower 5cm/2in of the remaining lemon grass stalk and discard; roughly chop the remaining lemon grass. Put it in a food processor with the remaining ginger, the onions, garlic, chillies and turmeric. Process to a smooth paste. Heat the oil in a frying pan and fry the paste until it gives off a rich aroma. Remove from the heat and add the fish.

3 Stir the coconut milk into the reserved fish stock, then add enough water to make up to 2.5 litres/4 pints/ 10 cups and pour into a large pan. In a jug, mix the rice flour and chick-pea (besan) flour to a thin cream with some of the stock. Stir this into the coconut and stock mixture and bring to the boil, stirring all the time.

4 Add the banana trunk or heart or bamboo shoots and cook for 10 minutes until just tender. Stir in the fish mixture and season. Cook until hot. Guests pour soup over the noodles and add hard-boiled egg, onions, spring onions, prawns and fried chillies as a garnish.

THAMIN LETHOK

THIS IS THE BURMESE WAY OF DEALING WITH LEFTOVERS, AND VERY SUCCESSFUL IT IS TOO. THE NOODLES AND RICE ARE ARRANGED ON PLATTERS WITH SOME OR ALL OF THE ACCOMPANIMENTS. EVERYTHING IS SERVED COLD, SO IT IS PERFECT FOR A SUMMER PARTY.

SERVES 6

INGREDIENTS
  175g/6oz/scant 1 cup long grain rice
  1–2 red chillies, seeded and
    roughly chopped
  1 small onion, roughly chopped
  15ml/1 tbsp vegetable oil
  350g/12oz potatoes, diced
  115g/4oz egg noodles, soaked for
    30 minutes in cold water to cover
  115g/4oz rice noodles, soaked for
    at least 10 minutes in cold water
    to cover
  50g/2oz cellophane noodles (or
    increase either of the above)
  225g/8oz spinach leaves
  175g/6oz/3 cups beansprouts
  25ml/1½ tbsp tamarind pulp or
    concentrate, soaked in 200ml/
    7fl oz/scant 1 cup warm water,
    or 6 lemon wedges
  salt

For the accompaniments
  1 very small onion, thinly sliced
  3 spring onions, finely shredded
  crisp fried onion
  50g/2oz cellophane noodles, fried
    until crisp
  25g/1oz/3 tbsp chick-peas, dry
    roasted and pounded
  3 dried chillies, dry-fried
    and pounded
  fresh coriander leaves

1 Bring a large pan of water to the boil and cook the rice for 12–15 minutes until tender. Drain, tip into a bowl and set aside. In a mortar, pound the chillies with the onion. Heat the oil in a small frying pan, add the mixture and fry for 2–3 minutes. Stir into the cooked rice.

2 Cook the potatoes in boiling salted water for about 8–10 minutes until just tender; drain and set aside. Drain the noodles and cook them in separate pans of salted, boiling water (see Cook's Tip). Drain, refresh under cold water and drain again.

3 Put the spinach into a large pan with just the water that clings to the leaves after washing. Cover the pan and cook for 2 minutes until starting to wilt. Drain well. Cook the beansprouts in the same way. Leave both to get cold.

COOK'S TIP
Cook noodles following the instructions on the packet: egg noodles need about 4 minutes and rice noodles are ready when the water boils again.

4 Arrange the cold flavoured rice, potato cubes, noodles, spinach and beansprouts attractively on a large serving platter. Set out the range of accompaniments. Strain the tamarind juice, if using, into a jug or put the lemon wedges on a plate. Each guest takes a little of whichever main ingredients they fancy, adds some accompaniments and drizzles over a little tamarind juice or a squeeze of lemon juice to taste.

INDONESIA

More than 13,000 islands make up this lush tropical archipelago. Numerous cultures
have flourished here, from the early Hindu and Buddhist empires to the rise of Islam.
In the following centuries, Portuguese and British merchants set up trading posts, but
the Dutch had the strongest impact, occupying the islands for 250 years. This culinary
heritage and the abundance of ingredients, such as rice, chillies, limes, tamarind and
spices, has led to the development of exciting dishes such as
Nasi Goreng, Gado-gado and Beef Rendang.

LAMB SATÉ

THESE TASTY LAMB SKEWERS ARE TRADITIONALLY SERVED WITH DAINTY DIAMOND-SHAPED PIECES OF COMPRESSED RICE, WHICH ARE SURPRISINGLY SIMPLE TO MAKE. OFFER THE REMAINING SAUCE FOR DIPPING.

MAKES 25–30 SKEWERS

INGREDIENTS
   1kg/2¼lb leg of lamb, boned
   3 garlic cloves, crushed
   15–30ml/1–2 tbsp chilli sambal or
      5–10ml/1–2 tsp chilli powder
   90ml/6 tbsp dark soy sauce
   juice of 1 lemon
   salt and ground black pepper
   groundnut or sunflower oil,
      for brushing

For the sauce
   6 garlic cloves, crushed
   15ml/1 tbsp chilli sambal or 2–3
      fresh chillies, seeded and ground
      to a paste
   90ml/6 tbsp dark soy sauce
   25ml/1½ tbsp lemon juice
   30ml/2 tbsp boiling water

To serve
   thinly sliced onion
   cucumber wedges (optional)
   compressed-rice shapes (see
      Cook's Tip)

1 Cut the lamb into neat 1cm/½in cubes. Remove any pieces of gristle, but do not trim off any of the fat because this keeps the meat moist during cooking and enhances the flavour. Spread out the lamb cubes in a single layer in a shallow bowl.

COOK'S TIP
Compressed rice shapes are easy to make. Cook two 115g/4oz packets if boil-in-the-bag rice in a large pan of salted, boiling water and simmer for 1¼ hours until the cooked rice fills each bag like a plump cushion. The bags must be covered with water throughout; use a saucer or plate to weigh them down. Let the bags cool completely before slitting them and removing the slabs of cooked rice. With a sharp, wetted knife, cut each rice slab horizontally in half, then into diamond shapes.

2 Put the garlic, chilli sambal or chilli powder, soy sauce and lemon juice in a mortar. Add salt and pepper and grind to a paste. Alternatively, process the mixture using a food processor. Pour over the lamb and mix to coat. Cover and leave in a cool place for at least 1 hour. Soak wooden or bamboo skewers in water to prevent them from scorching during cooking.

3 Prepare the sauce. Put the garlic into a bowl. Add the chilli sambal or fresh chillies, soy sauce, lemon juice and boiling water. Stir well. Preheat the grill. Thread the meat on to the skewers. Brush the skewered meat with oil and grill, turning often. Brush the saté with a little of the sauce and serve hot, with onion, cucumber wedges, if using, rice shapes and the sauce.

BALINESE VEGETABLE SOUP

THE BALINESE BASE THIS POPULAR SOUP ON BEANS, BUT ANY SEASONAL VEGETABLES CAN BE ADDED OR SUBSTITUTED. THE RECIPE ALSO INCLUDES SHRIMP PASTE, WHICH IS KNOWN LOCALLY AS TERASI.

2 Finely grind the chopped garlic, macadamia nuts or almonds, shrimp paste (blachan) and the coriander seeds to a paste using a pestle and mortar or in a food processor.

SERVES 8

INGREDIENTS
  225g/8oz green beans
  1.2 litres/2 pints/5 cups lightly
    salted water
  1 garlic clove, roughly chopped
  2 macadamia nuts or 4 almonds,
    finely chopped
  1cm/½ in cube shrimp paste
    (blachan)
  10–15ml/2–3 tsp coriander seeds,
    dry fried
  30ml/2 tbsp vegetable oil
  1 onion, finely sliced
  400ml/14fl oz can coconut milk
  2 bay leaves
  225g/8oz/4 cups beansprouts
  8 thin lemon wedges
  30ml/2 tbsp lemon juice
  salt and ground black pepper

1 Top and tail the beans, then cut them into small pieces. Bring the lightly salted water to the boil, add the beans to the pan and cook for 3–4 minutes. Drain, reserving the cooking water. Set the beans aside.

COOK'S TIP
Dry fry the coriander seeds for about 2 minutes until the aroma is released.

3 Heat the oil in a wok, and fry the onion until transparent. Remove with a slotted spoon. Add the nut paste to the wok and fry it for 2 minutes without allowing it to brown.

4 Pour in the reserved vegetable water. Spoon off 45–60ml/3–4 tbsp of the cream from the top of the coconut milk and set it aside. Add the remaining coconut milk to the wok, bring to the boil and add the bay leaves. Cook, uncovered, for 15–20 minutes.

5 Just before serving, reserve a few beans, fried onions and beansprouts for garnish and stir the rest into the soup. Add the lemon wedges, reserved coconut cream, lemon juice and seasoning; stir well. Pour into individual soup bowls and serve, garnished with reserved beans, onion and beansprouts.

SPICY SQUID

THIS AROMATICALLY SPICED SQUID DISH, CUMI CUMI SMOOR, IS SIMPLE YET DELICIOUS. GONE ARE THE DAYS WHEN CLEANING SQUID WAS SUCH A CHORE: TODAY THEY CAN BE BOUGHT READY-CLEANED FROM FISH SHOPS, MARKET STALLS AND THE FISH COUNTERS OF LARGE SUPERMARKETS.

2 Heat a wok and add 15ml/1 tbsp of the oil. When hot, toss in the squid strips and stir-fry for 2–3 minutes, by which time the squid will have curled into attractive shapes or into firm rings. Lift out and set aside.

3 Wipe out the wok, add the remaining oil and heat it. Stir-fry the onion and garlic until soft and beginning to brown. Stir in the tomato, soy sauce, nutmeg, cloves, water and lemon or lime juice. Bring to the boil, lower the heat and add the squid with seasoning to taste.

4 Cook the mixture gently for a further 3–5 minutes stirring from time to time to prevent sticking. Take care not to overcook the squid.

5 Divide boiled rice among 3–4 serving plates and spoon the spicy squid on top. Garnish with coriander leaves and shredded spring onions and serve.

SERVES 3–4

INGREDIENTS
675g/1½lb squid
45ml/3 tbsp groundnut oil
1 onion, finely chopped
2 garlic cloves, crushed
1 beefsteak tomato, peeled and chopped
15ml/1 tbsp dark soy sauce
2.5ml/½ tsp grated nutmeg
6 cloves
150ml/¼ pint/⅔ cup water
juice of ½ lemon or lime
salt and ground black pepper
fresh coriander leaves and shredded spring onion, to garnish
boiled rice, to serve

1 Rinse and drain the squid, then slice lengthways along one side and open it out flat. Score the inside of the squid in a lattice pattern, using the blunt side of a sharp knife, then cut it crossways into long thin strips.

NASI GORENG

ONE OF THE MOST FAMOUS INDONESIAN DISHES, THIS IS A MARVELLOUS WAY TO USE UP LEFTOVER RICE, CHICKEN AND MEATS. IT IS IMPORTANT THAT THE RICE BE QUITE COLD AND THE GRAINS SEPARATE BEFORE THE OTHER INGREDIENTS ARE ADDED, SO COOK THE RICE THE DAY BEFORE IF POSSIBLE.

SERVES 4–6

INGREDIENTS
  2 eggs
  30ml/2 tbsp water
  105ml/7 tbsp oil
  225g/8oz pork fillet or fillet of beef,
    cut into neat strips
  115g/4oz peeled cooked prawns,
    thawed if frozen
  175–225g/6–8oz cooked chicken,
    finely chopped
  2 fresh red chillies, halved
    and seeded
  1cm/½in cube shrimp paste
    (blachan)
  2 garlic cloves, crushed
  1 onion, roughly chopped
  675g/1½lb/6 cups cold cooked
    long grain rice, preferably
    basmati (about 350g/12oz/1¾ cups
    raw rice)
  30ml/2 tbsp dark soy sauce or
    45–60ml/3–4 tbsp tomato ketchup
  salt and ground black pepper
  deep-fried onions, celery leaves
    and fresh coriander sprigs,
    to garnish

1 Put the eggs in a bowl and beat in the water, with salt and pepper to taste. Using a non-stick frying pan make two or three omelettes using as little oil as possible for greasing. Roll up each omelette and cut in strips when cold. Set aside. Place the strips of pork or beef in a bowl. Put the prawns and chopped chicken in separate bowls. Shred one of the chillies and reserve it.

2 Put the shrimp paste (blachan) in a food processor. Add the remaining chilli, the garlic and the onion. Process to a fine paste. Alternatively, pound the mixture in a mortar, using a pestle.

3 Heat the remaining oil in a wok and fry the paste, without browning, until it gives off a rich, spicy aroma. Add the pork or beef and toss over the heat to seal in the juices, then cook for 2 minutes more, stirring constantly.

4 Add the prawns and stir-fry for 2 minutes. Finally, stir in the chicken, cold rice, dark soy sauce or ketchup and seasoning to taste. Reheat the rice fully, stirring all the time to keep the rice light and fluffy and prevent it from sticking to the base of the pan.

5 Spoon into individual dishes and arrange the omelette strips and reserved chilli on top. Garnish with the deep-fried onions and coriander sprigs.

SPICY MEAT BALLS

SERVE THESE SPICY LITTLE PATTIES — PERGEDEL DJAWA — *WITH EGG NOODLES AND CHILLI SAMBAL.*

SERVES 4–6

INGREDIENTS

    1cm/½in cube shrimp paste
      (blachan)
    1 large onion, roughly chopped
    1–2 fresh red chillies, seeded
      and chopped
    2 garlic cloves, crushed
    15ml/1 tbsp coriander seeds
    5ml/1 tsp cumin seeds
    450g/1lb lean minced beef
    10ml/2 tsp dark soy sauce
    5ml/1 tsp dark brown sugar
    juice of 1½ lemons
    a little beaten egg
    vegetable oil, for shallow frying
    salt and ground black pepper
    chilli sambal, to serve
    1 green and 2 fresh red chillies,
      to garnish

1 Wrap the shrimp paste (blachan) in a piece of foil and warm in a frying pan for 5 minutes, turning a few times. Unwrap and put in a food processor.

COOK'S TIP
When processing the shrimp paste (blachan), onion, chillies and garlic, do not process for too long, otherwise the onion will become too wet and spoil the consistency of the meat balls.

2 Add the onion, chillies and garlic to the food processor and process until finely chopped. Set aside. Dry fry the coriander and cumin seeds in a hot frying pan for 1 minute, to release the aroma. Tip the seeds into a mortar and grind with a pestle.

3 Put the meat in a large bowl. Stir in the onion mixture. Add the ground spices, soy sauce, brown sugar, lemon juice and beaten egg. Season to taste.

4 Shape the meat mixture into small, even-size balls, and chill these for 5–10 minutes to firm them up.

5 Heat the oil in a wok or large frying pan and fry the meat balls for 4–5 minutes, turning often, until cooked through and browned. You may have to do this in batches.

6 Drain the meat balls on kitchen paper, and then pile them on to a warm serving platter or into a large serving bowl. Finely slice the green chilli and one of the red chillies and scatter over the meat balls. Garnish with the remaining red chilli, if you like. Serve with the Chilli Sambal (see below) handed round separately.

VARIATION
Minced beef is traditionally used for this dish, but pork, lamb – or even turkey – mince would also be good.

CHILLI SAMBAL

THIS FIERCE CONDIMENT IS BOTTLED AS SAMBAL OELEK, *BUT IT IS EASY TO PREPARE AND WILL KEEP FOR SEVERAL WEEKS IN A WELL-SEALED JAR IN THE FRIDGE. USE A STAINLESS-STEEL OR PLASTIC SPOON TO MEASURE; IF SAUCE DRIPS ON YOUR FINGERS, WASH WELL IN SOAPY WATER* IMMEDIATELY.

MAKES 450G/1LB

INGREDIENTS

    450g/1lb fresh red chillies, seeded
    10ml/2 tsp salt

1 Bring a saucepan of water to the boil, add the seeded chillies and cook them for 5–8 minutes.

2 Drain the chillies and then grind them in a food processor, without making the paste too smooth.

3 Scrape into a screw-topped glass jar, stir in the salt and cover with a piece of greaseproof paper or clear film. Screw on the lid and store in the fridge. Spoon into small dishes, to serve as an accompaniment, or to use in recipes as suggested.

SWEET AND SOUR SALAD

ACAR BENING MAKES A PERFECT ACCOMPANIMENT TO A VARIETY OF SPICY DISHES AND CURRIES, WITH ITS CLEAN TASTE AND BRIGHT, JEWEL-LIKE COLOURS, AND POMEGRANATE SEEDS, THOUGH NOT TRADITIONAL, MAKE A BEAUTIFUL GARNISH. THIS IS AN ESSENTIAL DISH FOR A BUFFET PARTY.

SERVES 8

INGREDIENTS
- 1 small cucumber
- 1 onion, thinly sliced
- 1 small, ripe pineapple or 425g/ 15oz can pineapple rings
- 1 green pepper, seeded and thinly sliced
- 3 firm tomatoes, chopped
- 30ml/2 tbsp golden granulated sugar
- 45–60ml/3–4 tbsp white wine vinegar
- 120ml/4fl oz/1/2 cup water
- salt
- seeds of 1–2 pomegranates, to garnish

1 Halve the cucumber lengthways, remove the seeds, slice and spread on a plate with the onion. Sprinkle with salt. After 10 minutes, rinse and dry.

2 If using a fresh pineapple, peel and core it, removing all the eyes, then cut it into bite-size pieces. If using canned pineapple, drain the rings and cut them into small wedges. Place the pineapple in a bowl with the cucumber, onion, green pepper and tomatoes.

3 Heat the sugar, vinegar and measured water in a pan, stirring until the sugar has dissolved. Remove the pan from the heat and leave to cool. When cold, add a little salt to taste and pour over the fruit and vegetables. Cover and chill until required. Serve in small bowls, garnished with pomegranate seeds.

VARIATION
To make an Indonesian-style cucumber salad, salt a salad cucumber as described in the recipe. Make half the dressing and pour it over the cucumber. Add a few chopped spring onions. Cover and chill. Serve scattered with toasted sesame seeds.

FRUIT AND RAW VEGETABLE GADO-GADO

A BANANA LEAF, WHICH CAN BE BOUGHT FROM ASIAN STORES, CAN BE USED INSTEAD OF THE MIXED SALAD LEAVES TO LINE THE PLATTER FOR A SPECIAL OCCASION.

SERVES 6

INGREDIENTS
  1/2 cucumber
  2 pears (not too ripe) or 175g/6oz
    wedge of yam bean
  1–2 eating apples
  juice of 1/2 lemon
  mixed salad leaves
  6 small tomatoes, cut in wedges
  3 slices fresh pineapple, cored and
    cut in wedges
  3 eggs, hard-boiled and shelled
  175g/6oz egg noodles, cooked,
    cooled and chopped
  deep-fried onions, to garnish

For the peanut sauce
  2–4 fresh red chillies, seeded
    and ground, or 15ml/1 tbsp
    chilli sambal
  300ml/1/2 pint/1 1/4 cups
    coconut milk
  350g/12oz/1 1/4 cups crunchy
    peanut butter
  15ml/1 tbsp dark soy sauce or dark
    brown sugar
  5ml/1 tsp tamarind pulp, soaked in
    45ml/3 tbsp warm water
  coarsely crushed peanuts
  salt

2 Simmer gently until the sauce thickens, then stir in the soy sauce or sugar. Strain in the tamarind juice, add salt to taste and stir well. Spoon into a bowl and sprinkle with a few coarsely crushed peanuts.

VARIATION
Quail's eggs can be used instead of normal eggs and look very attractive in this dish. Hard boil for 3 minutes and halve or leave whole.

3 To make the salad, core the cucumber and peel the pears or yam bean. Cut them into matchsticks. Finely shred the apples and sprinkle them with the lemon juice. Spread a bed of lettuce leaves on a flat platter, then pile the fruit and vegetables on top.

4 Add the sliced or quartered hard-boiled eggs, the chopped noodles and the deep-fried onions. Serve at once, with the sauce.

1 Make the peanut sauce. Put the ground chillies or chilli sambal in a pan. Pour in the coconut milk, then stir in the peanut butter. Heat gently, stirring, until well blended.

BEEF RENDANG

IN INDONESIA, THIS SPICY DISH IS USUALLY SERVED WITH THE MEAT QUITE DRY; IF YOU PREFER MORE SAUCE, SIMPLY ADD MORE WATER WHEN STIRRING IN THE POTATOES.

SERVES 6–8

INGREDIENTS

2 onions or 5–6 shallots, chopped
4 garlic cloves, chopped
2.5cm/1in piece fresh galangal,
  peeled and sliced, or 15ml/1 tbsp
  galangal paste
2.5cm/1in piece fresh root ginger,
  peeled and sliced
4–6 fresh red chillies, seeded
  and roughly chopped
lower part only of 1 lemon grass
  stem, sliced
2.5cm/1in piece fresh turmeric,
  peeled and sliced, or 5ml/1 tsp
  ground turmeric
1kg/2¼lb prime beef in one piece
5ml/1 tsp coriander seeds, dry fried
5ml/1 tsp cumin seeds, dry fried
2 kaffir lime leaves, torn into pieces
2 x 400ml/14fl oz cans coconut milk
300ml/½ pint/1¼ cups water
30ml/2 tbsp dark soy sauce
5ml/1 tsp tamarind pulp, soaked in
  60ml/4 tbsp warm water
8–10 small new potatoes, scrubbed
salt and ground black pepper
deep-fried onions (see below),
  sliced fresh red chillies and spring
  onions, to garnish

1 Put the onions or shallots in a food processor. Add the garlic, galangal, ginger, chillies, sliced lemon grass and fresh or ground turmeric. Process to a fine paste or grind in a mortar, using a pestle.

2 Cut the meat into cubes using a large sharp knife, then place the cubes in a bowl.

3 Grind the dry-fried coriander and cumin seeds, then add to the meat with the onion, chilli paste and kaffir lime leaves; stir well. Cover and leave in a cool place to marinate while you prepare the other ingredients.

COOK'S TIP
This dish is even better if you can cook it a day or two in advance of serving, which allows the flavours to mellow beautifully. Add the potatoes on reheating and simmer until tender.

4 Pour the coconut milk and water into a wok, then stir in the spiced meat and the soy sauce. Strain the tamarind water and add to the wok. Stir over medium heat until the liquid boils, then simmer gently, half-covered, for 1½ hours.

5 Add the potatoes and simmer for 20–25 minutes, or until meat and potatoes are tender. Add water if liked. Season and serve, garnished with deep-fried onions, chillies and spring onions.

DEEP-FRIED ONIONS

KNOWN AS BAWANG GORENG, THESE ARE A TRADITIONAL GARNISH AND ACCOMPANY MANY INDONESIAN DISHES. ORIENTAL STORES SELL THEM READY-PREPARED, BUT IT IS EASY TO MAKE THEM. THE SMALL RED ONIONS SOLD IN ASIAN SHOPS ARE EXCELLENT AS THEY CONTAIN LESS WATER.

MAKES 450G/1LB

INGREDIENTS
450g/1lb onions
vegetable oil, for deep frying

1 Thinly slice the onions with a sharp knife or in a food processor. Spread the slices out in a single layer on kitchen paper and leave them to dry, in an airy place, for 30 minutes–2 hours.

2 Heat the oil in a deep fryer or wok to 190°C/375°F. Fry the onions in batches, until crisp and golden, turning all the time. Drain well on kitchen paper, cool and store in an airtight container, unless using immediately.

SAMBAL GORENG WITH PRAWNS

SAMBAL GORENG IS AN IMMENSELY USEFUL AND ADAPTABLE SAUCE. HERE IT IS COMBINED WITH PRAWNS AND GREEN PEPPER, BUT YOU COULD ADD FINE STRIPS OF CALF'S LIVER, CHICKEN LIVERS, TOMATOES, GREEN BEANS OR HARD-BOILED EGGS.

SERVES 4–6

INGREDIENTS
350g/12oz peeled cooked prawns
1 green pepper, seeded and thinly sliced
60ml/4 tbsp tamarind juice
pinch of sugar
45ml/3 tbsp coconut milk or cream
boiled rice, to serve
lime rind and red onion, to garnish

For the sambal goreng
2.5cm/1in cube shrimp paste (blachan)
2 onions, roughly chopped
2 garlic cloves, roughly chopped
2.5cm/1in piece fresh galangal, peeled and sliced
10ml/2 tsp chilli sambal or 2 fresh red chillies, seeded and sliced
1.5ml/¼ tsp salt
30ml/2 tbsp vegetable oil
45ml/3 tbsp tomato purée
600ml/1 pint/2½ cups vegetable stock or water

1 Make the sambal goreng. Grind the shrimp paste (blachan) with the onions and garlic using a mortar and pestle. Alternatively put in a food processor and process to a paste. Add the galangal, chilli sambal or sliced chillies and salt. Process or pound to a fine paste.

COOK'S TIP
Store the remaining sauce in the fridge for up to 3 days or freeze it for up to 3 months.

2 Heat the oil in a wok or frying pan and fry the paste for 1–2 minutes, without browning, until the mixture gives off a rich aroma. Stir in the tomato purée and the stock or water and cook for 10 minutes. Ladle half the sauce into a bowl and leave to cool. This leftover sauce can be used in another recipe (see Cook's Tip).

3 Add the prawns and green pepper to the remaining sauce. Cook over a medium heat for 3–4 minutes, then stir in the tamarind juice, sugar and coconut milk or cream. Spoon into warmed serving bowls and garnish with strips of lime rind and sliced red onion. Serve at once with boiled rice.

VARIATIONS
To make tomato sambal goreng, add 450g/1lb peeled coarsely chopped tomatoes to the sauce mixture, before stirring in the stock or water.
To make egg sambal goreng, add 3 or 4 chopped hard-boiled eggs, and 2 peeled chopped tomatoes to the sauce.

BAMIE GORENG

THIS FRIED NOODLE DISH IS WONDERFULLY ACCOMMODATING. YOU CAN ADD OTHER VEGETABLES, SUCH AS MUSHROOMS, TINY PIECES OF CHAYOTE, BROCCOLI, LEEKS OR BEANSPROUTS. USE WHATEVER IS TO HAND, BEARING IN MIND THE NEED FOR A BALANCE OF COLOURS, FLAVOURS AND TEXTURES.

SERVES 6–8

INGREDIENTS
 450g/1lb dried egg noodles
 2 eggs
 25g/1oz/2 tbsp butter
 90ml/6 tbsp vegetable oil
 1 skinless boneless chicken
  breast, sliced
 115g/4oz pork fillet, sliced
 115g/4oz calf's liver, finely
  sliced (optional)
 2 garlic cloves, crushed
 115g/4oz peeled cooked prawns
 115g/4oz pak-choi
 2 celery sticks, finely sliced
 4 spring onions, shredded
 about 60ml/4 tbsp chicken stock
 dark soy sauce and light soy sauce
 salt and ground black pepper
 deep-fried onions and shredded
  spring onions, to garnish (optional)

1 Bring a pan of lightly salted water to the boil, add the noodles and cook them for 3–4 minutes. Drain, rinse under cold water and drain again. Set aside.

2 Put the eggs in a bowl, beat and add salt and pepper to taste. Heat the butter with 5ml/1 tsp oil in a small pan, add the eggs and stir over a low heat until scrambled but still quite moist. Set aside.

3 Heat the remaining oil in a wok and fry the chicken, pork and liver (if using) with the garlic for 2–3 minutes, until the meat has changed colour. Add the prawns, pak-choi, sliced celery and shredded spring onions and toss to mix.

4 Add the noodles and toss over the heat until the prawns and noodles are heated through and the greens are lightly cooked. Add enough stock just to moisten and season with dark and light soy sauce to taste. Finally, add the scrambled eggs and toss to mix. Spoon on to a warmed serving platter or into individual dishes and serve at once, garnished with onions.

COOK'S TIP
Pak-choi is similar to Swiss chard and is available from Asian stores and large supermarkets.

BANANA FRITTERS

KNOWN AS PISANG GORENG, THESE DELICIOUS DEEP-FRIED BANANAS SHOULD BE COOKED AT THE LAST MINUTE, SO THAT THE BATTER IS CRISP AND THE BANANA INSIDE IS SOFT AND WARM.

SERVES 8

INGREDIENTS
115g/4oz/1 cup self-raising flour
40g/1½ oz/¼ cup rice flour
2.5ml/½ tsp salt
200ml/7fl oz/scant 1 cup water
finely grated lime rind (optional)
8 baby bananas
vegetable oil, for deep frying
strips of lime rind, to garnish
caster sugar and lime wedges,
   to serve

COOK'S TIP
Tiny bananas are available from some Asian stores and many larger supermarkets, alternatively use small bananas and cut in half lengthways and then in half again.

1 Sift together the self-raising flour, rice flour and salt into a bowl. Add just enough water to make a smooth, coating batter. Mix well, then add the lime rind, if using.

VARIATION
Instead of lime, add finely grated orange rind to the batter.

2 Heat the oil in a deep fryer or wok to 190°C/375°F. Meanwhile, peel the bananas. Dip them into the batter two or three times until well coated, then deep fry until crisp and golden. Drain on kitchen paper. Serve hot, dredged with the caster sugar and garnished with strips of lime. Offer the lime wedges for squeezing over the bananas.

BLACK GLUTINOUS RICE PUDDING

THIS VERY UNUSUAL RICE PUDDING, KNOWN AS BUBOR PULOT HITAM, IS FLAVOURED WITH BRUISED FRESH ROOT GINGER AND IS QUITE DELICIOUS SERVED WITH COCONUT MILK OR CREAM. WHEN COOKED, BLACK RICE STILL RETAINS ITS HUSK AND HAS A LOVELY NUTTY TEXTURE.

SERVES 6

INGREDIENTS
115g/4oz/⅔ cup black glutinous rice
475ml/16fl oz/2 cups water
1cm/½in piece fresh root ginger,
   peeled and bruised
50g/2oz/⅓ cup dark brown sugar
50g/2oz/¼ cup caster sugar
300ml/½ pint/1¼ cups coconut
   milk or coconut cream, to serve

COOK'S TIP
Canned coconut milk and cream is available, but it is easy to make at home. Blend 225g/8oz/2⅔ cups desiccated coconut with 450ml/¾ pint/1¾ cups boiling water in a food processor for 30 seconds, then cool slightly. Tip into a muslin-lined sieve and twist the muslin to extract as much liquid as possible.

1 Put the black glutinous rice in a sieve and rinse it well under plenty of cold running water. Drain the rice and put it in a large pan, along with the water. Bring the water to the boil and stir it as it heats, in order to prevent the rice from settling on the base of the pan. Cover the pan and cook over a very low heat for about 30 minutes.

2 Add the ginger and both types of sugar to the pan. Cook for 15 minutes more, adding a little more water if necessary, until the rice is cooked and porridge-like.

3 Remove the ginger and pour into individual bowls. Serve warm, topped with coconut milk or coconut cream.

VIETNAM AND THE PHILIPPINES

Vietnam borders China, Laos and Cambodia, in the heart of South-east Asia, and it is not surprising that its cuisine has much in common with its neighbours. In the north nearest China, stir-fries and mild curries are popular; further south there is a strong French influence. Rice, the staple, is bolstered by baguettes. Pâtés, herb salads, rare beef and casseroles feature alongside traditional dishes served with the pungent fish sauce, nuoc cham. In the Philippines, dishes such as Puchero, Escabeche and Adobo of Chicken owe much to their Spanish origins, but have their own distinct flavour.

VIETNAMESE RICE PAPER ROLLS

RICE PAPER WRAPPERS COME IN SMALL AND LARGE ROUNDS AND CAN BE BOUGHT FROM ASIAN SUPERMARKETS. THEY SOFTEN WHEN BRUSHED WITH WARM WATER, BUT THEY ARE VERY BRITTLE SO MUST BE HANDLED WITH CARE. CASUALTIES CAN BE USED FOR PATCHING OTHER PAPERS.

SERVES 8

INGREDIENTS
2 litres/3½ pints/8 cups water
1 small onion, sliced
a few fresh coriander stems
30ml/2 tbsp fish sauce
225g/8oz piece belly pork, boned and
   rind removed
50g/2oz fine rice vermicelli
225g/8oz/4 cups beansprouts, rinsed
   and drained
8 crisp lettuce leaves, halved
fresh mint and coriander leaves
175g/6oz peeled cooked prawns,
   thawed if frozen
16 large rice papers
ground black pepper

For the black bean sauce
15–30ml/1–2 tbsp groundnut oil
2 garlic cloves, crushed
1 fresh red chilli, seeded and sliced
60–75ml/4–5 tbsp canned black
   salted beans
30ml/2 tbsp fish sauce
5ml/1 tsp rice vinegar
10–15ml/2–3 tsp light brown sugar
15ml/1 tbsp crunchy peanut butter
15ml/1 tbsp sesame seeds, dry fried
5ml/1 tsp sesame oil
90ml/6 tbsp fish, pork or
   chicken stock

1 Mix the water, onion slices, coriander stems and fish sauce in a large pan. Bring to the boil. Add the pork and boil for 20–30 minutes, turning the pork from time to time until it is tender when tested with a skewer. Lift the pork from the pan, leave to cool, then slice it into thin strips. (Strain the stock and reserve it for making soup.)

2 Make the sauce. Heat the groundnut oil in a frying pan and fry the garlic and chilli for 1 minute. Stir in all the remaining ingredients, mix well, then transfer to a food processor and process briefly. Pour into a serving bowl and leave to cool.

3 Soak the rice vermicelli in warm water until softened. Drain well, then snip into neat lengths. Bring a pan of water to the boil and add the vermicelli. As soon as the water boils again, after about 1 minute, drain the noodles, rinse them under cold water, then drain them again. Put them in a serving bowl. Put the beansprouts in a separate dish, and arrange the lettuce and herb leaves on a platter. Put the prawns in a bowl.

4 When almost ready to serve place the rice papers two at a time on a dish towel and brush both sides with warm water to soften them.

5 Transfer two rice papers very carefully to each of eight individual serving plates. Each guest places a piece of lettuce on a rice paper wrapper at the end closest to them, topping it with some of the noodles and beansprouts, a few mint or coriander leaves and some strips of pork.

6 Roll up one turn and then place a few prawns on the open part of the wrapper. Continue rolling to make a neat parcel. The roll can be cut in half, if preferred, then it is dipped in the black bean sauce before being eaten. The second wrapper is filled and eaten in the same way.

CHA GIO AND NUOC CHAM

CHINESE SPRING ROLL WRAPPERS ARE USED HERE INSTEAD OF THE RICE PAPERS TRADITIONALLY USED IN VIETNAM. CHA GIO IS AN IMMENSELY POPULAR SNACK — THE VEGETABLE CONTENT OF THE FILLING CAN BE VARIED AS LONG AS THE FLAVOURS ARE COMPLEMENTARY.

<u>MAKES 15</u>

INGREDIENTS
  25g/1oz cellophane noodles soaked
    for 10 minutes in hot water to cover
  6–8 dried wood ears, soaked for
    30 minutes in warm water to cover
  225g/8oz minced pork
  225g/8oz fresh or canned crab meat
  4 spring onions, trimmed and
    finely chopped
  5ml/1 tsp fish sauce
  flour and water paste, to seal
  250g/9oz packet spring roll wrappers
  vegetable oil, for deep frying
  salt and ground black pepper

For the *nuoc cham* sauce
  2 fresh red chillies, seeded and
    pounded to a paste
  2 garlic cloves, crushed
  15ml/1 tbsp sugar
  45ml/3 tbsp fish sauce
  juice of 1 lime or ½ lemon

1 Make the *nuoc cham* sauce by mixing the chillies, garlic, sugar and fish sauce in a bowl and stirring in lime or lemon juice to taste. Drain the noodles and snip into 2.5cm/1in lengths. Drain the wood ears, trim away any rough stems and slice the wood ears finely.

COOK'S TIP
Serve the rolls Vietnamese-style by wrapping each roll in a lettuce leaf together with a few sprigs of fresh mint and coriander and a stick of cucumber.

2 Mix the noodles and the wood ears with the pork and set aside. Remove any cartilage from the crab meat and add to the pork mixture with the spring onions and fish sauce. Season to taste, mixing well.

3 Place a spring roll wrapper in front of you, diamond-fashion. Spoon some mixture just below the centre, fold over the nearest point and roll once.

4 Fold in the sides to enclose, then brush the edges with flour paste and roll up to seal. Repeat with the remaining wrappers and filling.

5 Heat the oil in a wok or deep fryer to 190°C/375°F. Deep fry the rolls in batches for 8–10 minutes or until they are cooked through. Drain them well on kitchen paper and serve hot. To eat, dip the rolls in the *nuoc cham* sauce.

CHICKEN, VEGETABLE AND CHILLI SALAD

GOI TOM, A TYPICAL VIETNAMESE SALAD, IS FULL OF SURPRISING TEXTURES AND FLAVOURS. SERVE AS A LIGHT LUNCH DISH OR FOR SUPPER WITH CRUSTY FRENCH BREAD.

SERVES 4

INGREDIENTS
  225g/8oz Chinese leaves
  2 carrots, cut in matchsticks
  1/2 cucumber, cut in matchsticks
  salt
  2 fresh red chillies, seeded and cut
    into thin strips
  1 small onion, sliced into fine rings
  4 pickled gherkins, sliced, plus
    45ml/3 tbsp of the liquid
  50g/2oz/1/2 cup peanuts,
    lightly ground
  225g/8oz cooked chicken,
    finely sliced
  1 garlic clove, crushed
  5ml/1 tsp sugar
  30ml/2 tbsp cider or white vinegar

1 Finely slice the Chinese leaves and set aside with the carrot matchsticks. Spread out the cucumber matchsticks on a board and sprinkle with salt. Set aside for 15 minutes.

COOK'S TIP
Add a little more cider or white wine vinegar to the dressing if a sharper taste is preferred.

2 Mix together the chillies and onion rings and then add the sliced gherkins and peanuts. Tip the salted cucumber into a colander, rinse well and pat dry.

3 Put all the vegetables into a salad bowl and add the chilli mixture and chicken. Mix the gherkin liquid with the garlic, sugar and vinegar. Pour over the salad, toss lightly and serve.

ASPARAGUS AND CRAB SOUP

ASPARAGUS OWES ITS POPULARITY TO THE FRENCH INFLUENCE ON VIETNAMESE COOKING. IT IS OFTEN COMBINED WITH CRAB AND MADE INTO A DELICIOUS SOUP, CAHN CUA.

SERVES 4–6

INGREDIENTS
  350g/12oz asparagus spears,
    trimmed and halved
  900ml/1 1/2 pints/3 3/4 cups chicken
    stock, preferably home-made
  30–45ml/2–3 tbsp sunflower oil
  6 shallots, chopped
  115g/4oz crab meat, fresh or
    canned, chopped
  15ml/1 tbsp cornflour, mixed to a
    paste with water
  30ml/2 tbsp fish sauce
  1 egg, lightly beaten
  snipped chives, plus extra chives
    to garnish
  salt and ground black pepper to taste

1 Cook the asparagus spears in the chicken stock for 5–6 minutes until tender. Drain, reserving the stock.

2 Heat the oil in a large wok or frying pan and stir-fry the chopped shallots for 2 minutes, without allowing them to brown. Add the asparagus spears, chopped crab meat and chicken stock.

3 Bring the mixture to the boil and cook for 3 minutes, then remove the wok or pan from the heat and spoon some of the liquid into the cornflour mixture. Return this to the wok or pan and stir until the soup begins to thicken slightly.

4 Stir in the fish sauce, with salt and pepper to taste, then pour the beaten egg into the soup, stirring briskly so that the egg forms threads. Finally, stir the snipped chives into the soup and serve it immediately, garnished with chives.

COOK'S TIP
If fresh asparagus isn't available, use 350g/12oz can asparagus. Drain and halve the spears.

FILIPINO PRAWN FRITTERS

UKOY ARE A FAVOURITE SNACK OR STARTER. UNUSUALLY, THEY ARE FIRST SHALLOW FRIED, THEN DEEP FRIED. THEY ARE BEST EATEN FRESH FROM THE PAN, FIRST DIPPED IN THE PIQUANT SAUCE.

4 Peel and grate the sweet potato using the large holes on a grater, and add it to the batter, then stir in the crushed garlic and the drained beansprouts.

5 Pour the oil for shallow frying into a large frying pan. It should be about 5mm/¼in deep. Pour more oil into a wok for deep frying. Heat the oil in the frying pan. Taking a generous spoonful of the batter, drop it carefully into the frying pan so that it forms a fritter, about the size of a large drop scone.

6 Make more fritters in the same way. As soon as the fritters have set, top each one with a single prawn and a few chopped spring onions. Continue to cook over a medium heat for 1 minute, then remove with a fish slice.

7 Heat the oil in the wok to 190°C/ 375°F and deep fry the prawn fritters in batches until they are crisp and golden brown. Drain the fritters on absorbent kitchen paper and then arrange on a serving plate or platter. Offer a bowl of the sauce for dipping.

SERVES 2–4

INGREDIENTS
    16 raw prawns in the shell
    225g/8oz/2 cups plain flour
    5ml/1 tsp baking powder
    2.5ml/½ tsp salt
    1 egg, beaten
    1 small sweet potato
    1 garlic clove, crushed
    115g/4oz/2 cups beansprouts, soaked
      in cold water and well drained
    vegetable oil, for shallow and
      deep frying
    4 spring onions, chopped

For the dipping sauce
    1 garlic clove, sliced
    45ml/3 tbsp rice or wine vinegar
    15–30ml/1–2 tbsp water
    salt, to taste
    6–8 small red chillies

1 Mix together all the ingredients for the dipping sauce and divide between two small bowls.

2 Put the whole prawns in a pan with water to cover. Bring to the boil, then simmer for 4–5 minutes or until the prawns are pink and tender. Lift the prawns from the pan with a slotted spoon. Discard the heads and the body shell, but leave the tails on. Strain and reserve the cooking liquid. Allow to cool.

3 Sift the flour, baking powder and salt into a bowl. Add the beaten egg and about 300ml/½ pint/1¼ cups of the prawn stock to make a batter that has the consistency of double cream.

VARIATION
Use cooked tiger prawns if you prefer. In this case, make the batter using fish stock or chicken stock.

ESCABECHE

THIS PICKLED FISH DISH IS EATEN WHEREVER THERE ARE — OR HAVE BEEN — SPANISH SETTLERS. HERE IT HAS BEEN MODIFIED IN ORDER TO REFLECT THE CHINESE INFLUENCE ON FILIPINO CUISINE.

SERVES 6

INGREDIENTS

675–900g/1½–2lb white fish fillets, such as sole or plaice
45–60ml/3–4 tbsp seasoned flour
vegetable oil, for shallow frying

For the sauce
2.5cm/1in piece fresh root ginger, peeled and thinly sliced
2–3 garlic cloves, crushed
1 onion, cut into thin rings
30ml/2 tbsp vegetable oil
½ large green pepper, seeded and cut in small neat squares
½ large red pepper, seeded and cut in small neat squares
1 carrot, cut into matchsticks
25ml/1½ tbsp cornflour
450ml/¾ pint/scant 2 cups water
45–60ml/3–4 tbsp herb or cider vinegar
15ml/1 tbsp light soft brown sugar
5–10ml/1–2 tsp fish sauce
salt and ground black pepper
1 small chilli, seeded and sliced and spring onions, finely shredded, to garnish (optional)
boiled rice, to serve

1 Wipe the fish fillets and leave them whole, or cut into serving portions, if you like. Pat dry on kitchen paper then dust lightly with seasoned flour.

2 Heat oil for shallow frying in a frying pan and fry the fish in batches until golden and almost cooked. Transfer to an ovenproof dish and keep warm.

3 Make the sauce in a wok or large frying pan. Fry the ginger, garlic and onion in the oil for 5 minutes or until the onion is softened but not browned.

4 Add the pepper squares and carrot strips and stir-fry for 1 minute.

5 Put the cornflour in a small bowl and add a little of the water to make a paste. Stir in the remaining water, the vinegar and the sugar. Pour the cornflour mixture over the vegetables in the wok and stir until the sauce boils and thickens a little. Season with fish sauce and salt and pepper if needed.

6 Add the fish to the sauce and reheat briefly without stirring. Transfer to a warmed serving platter and garnish with chilli and spring onions, if liked. Serve with boiled rice.

COOK'S TIP
Red snapper or small sea bass could be used for this recipe, in which case ask your fishmonger to cut them into fillets.

ADOBO OF CHICKEN AND PORK

FOUR INGREDIENTS ARE ESSENTIAL IN AN ADOBO, ONE OF THE BEST-LOVED RECIPES IN THE FILIPINO REPERTOIRE. THEY ARE VINEGAR, GARLIC, PEPPERCORNS AND BAY LEAVES.

SERVES 4

INGREDIENTS
    1 chicken, about 1.4kg/3lb, or
      4 chicken quarters
    350g/12oz pork leg steaks (with fat)
    10ml/2 tsp sugar
    60ml/4 tbsp sunflower oil
    75ml/5 tbsp wine or cider vinegar
    4 plump garlic cloves, crushed
    ¹/₂ tsp black peppercorns,
      crushed lightly
    15ml/1 tbsp light soy sauce
    4 bay leaves
    2.5ml/¹/₂ tsp annatto seeds, soaked
      in 30ml /2 tbsp boiling water, or
      2.5ml/¹/₂ tsp ground turmeric
    salt

For the plantain chips
    1–2 large plantains and/or
      1 sweet potato
    vegetable oil, for deep frying

1 Wipe the chicken and cut into eight even-size pieces, or halve the chicken quarters, if using. Cut the pork into neat pieces. Spread out all the meat on a board, sprinkle lightly with sugar and set aside.

2 Heat the oil in a wok or large frying pan and fry the chicken and pork pieces, in batches if necessary, until they are golden on both sides.

3 Add the vinegar, garlic, peppercorns, soy sauce and bay leaves and stir well.

4 Strain the annatto seed liquid and stir it into the pan or stir in the turmeric. Add salt to taste. Bring to the boil, cover, lower the heat and simmer for 30–35 minutes. Remove the lid and simmer for 10 minutes more.

5 Meanwhile, prepare the plaintain chips. Heat the oil in a deep fryer to 195°C/390°F. Peel the plantains or sweet potato (or both), if you like, and slice them into rounds or chips. Deep fry them, in batches if necessary, until cooked but not brown. Drain on kitchen paper. When ready to serve, reheat the oil and fry the plantains or sweet potato until crisp – it will only take a few seconds. Drain. Spoon the adobo into a serving dish and serve with the chips.

COOK'S TIP
Sprinkling the chicken lightly with sugar turns the skin beautifully brown when fried, but do not have the oil too hot to begin with or they will over-brown.

SINIGANG

MANY FILIPINOS WOULD CONSIDER THIS SOURED SOUP-LIKE STEW TO BE THEIR NATIONAL DISH. IT IS ALWAYS SERVED WITH NOODLES OR RICE, AND FISH — PRAWNS OR THIN SLIVERS OF FISH FILLET — IS OFTEN ADDED FOR GOOD MEASURE.

3 Pour the prepared fish stock into a large saucepan and add the diced mooli. Cook the mooli for 5 minutes, then add the beans and continue to cook for 3–5 minutes more.

SERVES 4–6

INGREDIENTS
15ml/1 tbsp tamarind pulp
150ml/1/4 pint/2/3 cup warm water
2 tomatoes
115g/4oz spinach or Chinese
  kangkong leaves
115g/4oz peeled cooked large
  prawns, thawed if frozen
1.2 litres/2 pints/5 cups prepared
  fish stock (see Cook's Tip)
1/2 mooli, peeled and finely diced
115g/4oz green beans, cut into
  1cm/1/2in lengths
225g/8oz piece of cod or haddock
  fillet, skinned and cut into strips
fish sauce, to taste
squeeze of lemon juice, to taste
salt and ground black pepper
boiled rice or noodles, to serve

1 Put the tamarind pulp in a bowl and pour over the warm water. Set aside while you peel and chop the tomatoes, discarding the seeds. Strip the spinach or kangkong leaves from the stems and tear into small pieces.

2 Remove the heads and shells from the prawns, leaving the tails intact.

4 Add the fish strips, tomato and spinach. Strain in the tamarind juice and cook for 2 minutes. Stir in the prawns and cook for 1–2 minutes to heat. Season with salt and pepper and add a little fish sauce and lemon juice to taste. Transfer to individual serving bowls and serve immediately, with rice or noodles.

COOK'S TIP
A good fish stock is essential for Sinigang. Ask your fishmonger for about 675g/11/2lb fish bones. Wash them, then place in a large pan with 2 litres/31/2 pints/8 cups water. Add half a peeled onion, a piece of bruised peeled ginger, and a little salt and pepper. Bring to the boil, skim, then simmer for 20 minutes. Cool slightly, then strain. Freeze unused fish stock.

PUCHERO

A FILIPINO POT-AU-FEU WITH SPANISH CONNECTIONS. SOMETIMES IT IS SERVED AS TWO COURSES, FIRST SOUP, THEN MEAT AND VEGETABLES WITH RICE, BUT IT CAN HAPPILY BE SERVED AS IS, ON RICE IN A WIDE SOUP BOWL. EITHER WAY IT IS VERY SATISFYING AND A SIESTA AFTERWARDS IS RECOMMENDED.

SERVES 6–8

INGREDIENTS
225g/8oz/generous 1 cup chick-peas, soaked overnight in water to cover
1.4kg/3lb chicken, cut into 8 pieces
350g/12oz belly of pork, rinded, or pork fillet, cubed
2 chorizo sausages, thickly sliced
2 onions, chopped
2.5 litres/4 pints/10 cups water
60ml/4 tbsp vegetable oil
2 garlic cloves, crushed
3 large tomatoes, peeled, seeded and chopped
15ml/1 tbsp tomato purée
1–2 sweet potatoes, cut into 1cm/1/2in cubes
2 plantains, sliced (optional)
salt and ground black pepper
chives or chopped spring onions, to garnish
1/2 head Chinese leaves, shredded, and boiled rice, to serve

For the aubergine sauce
1 large aubergine
3 garlic cloves, crushed
60–90ml/4–6 tbsp wine or cider vinegar

1 Drain the chick-peas and put them in a large saucepan. Cover with water, bring to the boil and boil rapidly for 10 minutes. Reduce the heat and simmer for 30 minutes until the chick-peas are half tender. Drain.

2 Put the chicken pieces, pork, sausage and half of the onions in a large pan. Add the chick-peas and pour in the water. Bring to the boil and lower the heat, cover and simmer for 1 hour or until the meat is just tender when tested with a skewer.

3 Meanwhile, make the aubergine sauce. Preheat the oven to 200°C/400°F/Gas 6. Prick the aubergine in several places, then place it on a baking sheet and bake for 30 minutes or until very soft.

4 Cool slightly, then peel away the aubergine skin and scrape the flesh into a bowl. Mash the flesh with the crushed garlic, season to taste and add enough vinegar to sharpen the sauce, which should be quite piquant. Set aside.

5 Heat the oil in a frying pan and fry the remaining onion and garlic for 5 minutes, until soft but not brown. Stir in the tomatoes and tomato purée and cook for 2 minutes, then add this mixture to a large pan with the diced sweet potato. Add the plantains, if using. Cook over a gentle heat for about 20 minutes until the sweet potato is thoroughly cooked. Add the Chinese leaves for the last minute or two.

6 Spoon the thick meat soup into a soup tureen, and put the vegetables in a separate serving bowl. Garnish both with whole or chopped chives or spring onions and serve with boiled rice and the aubergine sauce.

ENSAIMADAS

THESE SWEET BREAD ROLLS ARE A POPULAR SNACK IN THE PHILIPPINES AND COME WITH VARIOUS FILLINGS, SEVERAL OF THEM SAVOURY. THIS VERSION INCLUDES CHEESE.

MAKES 10–12

INGREDIENTS
  30ml/2 tbsp caster sugar, plus extra
    for sprinkling
  150ml/¼ pint/⅔ cup warm water
  15ml/1 tbsp dried active yeast
  450g/1lb/4 cups strong white flour
  5ml/1 tsp salt
  115g/4oz/½ cup butter, softened,
    plus 30ml/2 tbsp melted butter for
    the filling
  4 egg yolks
  90–120ml/6–8 tbsp warm milk
  115g/4oz/1 cup grated Cheddar
    cheese (or similar well-flavoured
    hard cheese)

1 Dissolve 5ml/1 tsp of the sugar in the warm water, then sprinkle in the dried yeast. Stir, then set aside for 10 minutes or until frothy. Sift the flour and salt into a large bowl.

2 Cream the softened butter with the remaining sugar in a large bowl. When it is fluffy, beat in the egg yolks and a little of the sifted flour. Gradually stir in the remaining flour with the yeast mixture and enough milk to form a soft but not sticky dough. Transfer to an oiled plastic bag. Close the bag loosely, leaving plenty of room for the dough to rise. Leave in a warm place for about 1 hour, until the dough doubles in bulk.

3 On a lightly floured surface, knock back the dough, then roll it out into a large rectangle. Brush the surface with half the melted butter, scatter with the cheese, then roll up from a long side like a Swiss roll.

4 Knead the dough thoroughly to distribute the cheese, then divide the dough into 10–12 pieces.

5 Roll each piece of dough into a thin rope, about 38cm/15in long. On greased baking sheets, coil each rope into a loose spiral, spacing them well apart. Tuck the loose ends under to seal. Leave to rise, in a warm place, for about 45 minutes or until doubled in size. Meanwhile, preheat the oven to 220°C/425°F/Gas 7.

6 Bake the ensaimadas in the oven for 15–20 minutes, until golden and cooked through. Remove from the oven, then immediately brush with the remaining melted butter and sprinkle with caster sugar. Serve warm.

CHURROS

THESE IRRESISTIBLE FRITTERS, SERVED AT EVERY OPPORTUNITY WITH HOT CHOCOLATE OR COFFEE, CAME TO THE PHILIPPINES WITH THE SPANISH WHO WERE KEEN TO KEEP MEMORIES OF HOME ALIVE.

MAKES ABOUT 24

INGREDIENTS
  450ml/15fl oz/scant 2 cups water
  15ml/1 tbsp olive oil
  15ml/1 tbsp sugar, plus extra
    for sprinkling
  2.5ml/½ tsp salt
  150g/5oz/1¼ cups plain flour
  1 large egg
  sunflower oil, for deep frying
  caster sugar, for sprinkling

COOK'S TIP
If you don't have a piping bag, you could fry teaspoons of mixture in the same way. Don't try to fry too many churros at a time as they swell a little during cooking.

1 Mix the water, oil, sugar and salt in a large pan and bring to the boil. Remove from the heat, and then sift in the flour. Beat well with a wooden spoon until smooth.

2 Beat in the egg to make a smooth, glossy mixture with a piping consistency. Spoon into a pastry bag fitted with a large star nozzle.

3 Heat the oil in a wok or deep fryer to 190°C/375°F. Pipe loops of the mixture, two at a time, into the hot oil. Cook the loops for 3–4 minutes until they are golden.

4 Lift out the churros with a wire skimmer or slotted spoon and drain them on kitchen paper. Dredge them with caster sugar and serve warm.

LECHE FLAN

SERVE THIS DELICIOUS DESSERT HOT OR COLD WITH WHIPPED CREAM OR CRÈME FRAÎCHE. THE USE OF EVAPORATED MILK REFLECTS THE 50 YEARS OF AMERICAN PRESENCE IN THE PHILIPPINES.

SERVES 8

INGREDIENTS
  5 large eggs
  30ml/2 tbsp caster sugar
  few drops vanilla essence
  410g/14½oz can evaporated milk
  300ml/½ pint/1¼ cups milk
  5ml/1 tsp finely grated lime rind
  strips of lime rind, to decorate

For the caramel
  225g/8oz/1 cup sugar
  120ml/4fl oz/½ cup water

1 Make the caramel. Put the sugar and water in a heavy-based pan. Stir to dissolve the sugar, then boil without stirring until golden. Quickly pour into eight ramekins, rotating them to coat the sides. Set aside to set.

2 Preheat the oven to 150°C/300°F/ Gas 2. Beat the eggs, sugar and vanilla essence in a bowl. Mix the evaporated milk and fresh milk in a pan. Heat to just below boiling point, then pour on to the egg mixture, stirring all the time. Strain the custard mixture into a jug, add the grated lime rind and cool. Pour into the caramel-coated ramekins.

3 Place the ramekins in a roasting tin and pour in enough warm water to come halfway up the sides of the dishes.

4 Transfer the roasting tin to the oven and cook the custards for 35–45 minutes or until they just shimmer when the ramekins are gently shaken.

5 Serve the custards in their ramekin dishes or by inverting on to serving plates, in which case break the caramel and use as decoration. The custards can be served warm or cold, decorated with strips of lime rind.

COOK'S TIP
Make extra caramel, if you like, for a garnish. Pour on to lightly oiled foil and leave to set, then crush with a rolling pin.

JAPAN AND KOREA

Japanese food is unique. The 200 year ban on foreigners from 1640 meant that food
in Japan remained true to its origins and exquisitely refined. Artistry is evident in even
the simplest dish. Eating out is the norm, and restaurants specialize in dishes such as
Sushi, Sukiyaki, Sashimi or Tempura. Korean food features seven basic flavours — garlic,
ginger, pepper, soy sauce, spring onions, sesame oil and toasted sesame seeds.

SASHIMI

THIS JAPANESE SPECIALITY — SLICED RAW FISH — EMPLOYS THE CUTTING TECHNIQUE KNOWN AS HIRA ZUKURI. THE PERFECTLY CUT FISH CAN BE ARRANGED IN MANY ATTRACTIVE WAYS AND IS THEN SERVED WITH WASABI — JAPANESE HORSERADISH — AND SOY SAUCE.

SERVES 4

INGREDIENTS
  2 fresh salmon fillets, skinned and
    any stray bones removed, total
    weight about 400g/14oz
  Japanese soy sauce and wasabi
    paste, to serve

For the garnish
  50g/2oz mooli, peeled
  shiso leaves

1 Put the salmon fillets in a freezer for 10 minutes to make them easier to cut, then lay them skinned side up with the thick end to your right and away from you. Use a long sharp knife and tilt it to the left. Slice carefully towards you, starting the cut from the point of the knife, then slide the slice away from the fillet, to the right. Always slice from the far side towards you.

2 Finely shred or grate the mooli and place in a bowl of cold water. Leave for 5 minutes, then drain well.

3 Arrange the salmon in an attractive way on a serving platter, or divide the salmon among four serving plates.

4 Give guests their own platter, together with a garnish of mooli and shiso leaves. The fish is eaten dipped in soy sauce and wasabi paste.

COOK'S TIP
Salmon and tuna are among the most popular choices for sashimi, although almost any type of fish can be used. If you are making sashimi for the first time, choose salmon or tuna and make sure you buy from a reputable fishmonger where you can be sure the fish is absolutely fresh.

YAKITORI CHICKEN

*THESE ARE JAPANESE-STYLE KEBABS. THEY ARE EASY TO EAT AND IDEAL FOR BARBECUES OR PARTIES.
MAKE EXTRA YAKITORI SAUCE IF YOU WOULD LIKE TO SERVE IT WITH THE KEBABS.*

SERVES 4

INGREDIENTS
6 boneless chicken thighs
bunch of spring onions
shichimi (seven-flavour spice), to
   serve (optional)

For the yakitori sauce
150ml/^{1}/$_4$ pint/^{2}/$_3$ cup Japanese
   soy sauce
90g/3^1/$_2$oz/scant ^{1}/$_2$ cup sugar
25ml/1^1/$_2$ tbsp sake or dry
   white wine
15ml/1 tbsp plain flour

3 Cut the spring onions into 3cm/
1^1/$_4$in pieces. Preheat the grill or light
the barbecue.

4 Thread the chicken and spring
onions alternately on to the drained
skewers. Grill under medium heat or
cook on the barbecue, brushing
generously several times with the sauce.
Allow 5–10 minutes, until the chicken is
cooked but still moist.

5 Serve with a little extra yakitori
sauce, offering shichimi (seven-flavour
spice) with the kebabs if available.

COOK'S TIP
Paprika can be used instead of shichimi,
if that is difficult to obtain.

1 Soak 12 bamboo skewers in water for
at least 30 minutes to prevent them
from scorching under the grill. Make the
sauce. Stir the soy sauce, sugar and
sake or wine into the flour in a small
saucepan and bring to the boil, stirring.
Lower the heat and simmer the mixture
for 10 minutes, until the sauce is
reduced by a third. Set aside.

2 Cut each chicken thigh into bite-size
pieces and set aside.

CHICKEN AND EGG WITH RICE

OYAKO-DON, THE JAPANESE NAME FOR THIS DISH MEANS PARENT (OYA), CHILD (KO) AND BOWL (DON); IT IS SO CALLED BECAUSE IT USES BOTH CHICKEN MEAT AND EGG. A CLASSIC DISH, IT IS EATEN THROUGHOUT THE YEAR.

2 Place the onion, dashi, sugar, soy sauce and mirin (sweet rice wine) in a saucepan and bring to the boil. Add the chicken and cook over a medium heat for about 5 minutes, or until cooked. Skim off any scum that rises to the surface of the liquid.

3 Ladle a quarter of the chicken and stock mixture into a frying pan and heat until the liquid comes to the boil.

SERVES 4

INGREDIENTS
   300g/11oz skinless boneless
     chicken breasts
   1 large mild onion, thinly sliced
   200ml/7fl oz/scant 1 cup freshly
     made dashi (kombu and bonito
     stock) or instant dashi
   22.5ml/4½ tsp sugar
   60ml/4 tbsp Japanese soy sauce
   30ml/2 tbsp mirin (sweet rice wine)
   4 eggs, beaten
   60ml/4 tbsp frozen peas, thawed
   boiled rice, to serve

1 Slice the chicken breasts diagonally with a sharp knife, then cut the slices into 3cm/1¼ in lengths.

4 Pour a quarter of the beaten egg over the mixture in the frying pan and sprinkle over 15ml/1 tbsp of the peas.

5 Cover and cook over a medium heat until the egg is just set. Slide the egg mixture on to a large plate and keep it warm while cooking the other omelettes in the same way. Transfer to serving dishes and serve with boiled rice.

COOK'S TIP
Ideally use either Japanese rice or Thai fragrant rice for this meal and allow 50–75g/2–3oz raw rice per person.

RICE TRIANGLES

PICNICS ARE VERY POPULAR IN JAPAN AND RICE SHAPES — ONIGIRI — ARE IDEAL PICNIC FARE.
YOU CAN PUT ANYTHING YOU LIKE IN THE RICE, SO YOU COULD INVENT YOUR OWN ONIGIRI.

SERVES 4

INGREDIENTS
1 salmon steak
15ml/1 tbsp salt
450g/1lb/4 cups freshly cooked
   sushi rice
4 umeboshi (plum pickles)
1/2 sheet yaki-nori seaweed, cut into
   four equal strips
white and black sesame seeds,
   for sprinkling

1 Grill the salmon steak for 4–5 minutes on each side, until the flesh flakes easily when it is tested with the tip of a sharp knife. Set aside to cool while you make other *onigiri*. When the salmon is cold, flake it, discarding any skin and bones.

2 Put the salt in a bowl. Spoon a quarter of the warm cooked rice into a small rice bowl. Make a hole in the middle of the rice and put in one umeboshi. Smooth the rice over to cover.

3 Wet the palms of both hands with cold water, then rub the salt evenly on to your palms.

4 Empty the rice and umeboshi from the bowl on to one hand. Use both hands to shape the rice into a triangular shape, using firm but not heavy pressure. Make three more rice triangles in the same way.

5 Mix the flaked salmon into the remaining rice, then shape it into triangles as before.

6 Wrap a strip of yaki-nori around each of the umeboshi triangles. Sprinkle sesame seeds on the salmon triangles.

COOK'S TIP
Always use warm rice to make the triangles. Allow them to cool completely and wrap each in foil or clear film.

MISO SOUP

THIS SOUP IS ONE OF THE MOST COMMONLY EATEN DISHES IN JAPAN, AND IT IS USUALLY SERVED WITH EVERY MEAL THAT INCLUDES RICE.

SERVES 4

INGREDIENTS
^{1}/$_2$ packet silken beancurd (tofu), drained weight about 150g/5oz
1 litre/1^3/$_4$ pints/4 cups freshly made dashi (kombu and bonito stock) or instant dashi
10g/^{1}/$_4$oz dried wakame seaweed
60ml/4 tbsp white or red miso paste
2 spring onions, shredded, to garnish

COOK'S TIP
Reduce the heat when the stock boils, as the delicate flavour of the soup will be lost if it is boiled for too long.

1 Cut the beancurd into 1cm/^{1}/$_2$in cubes. Bring the dashi to the boil, lower the heat and add the wakame seaweed. Simmer for 1–2 minutes.

2 Pour a little of the soup into a bowl and add the miso paste, stirring until it dissolves. Pour the mixture back into the pan.

3 Add the beancurd and heat through for 1 minute. Pour the soup into warmed serving dishes and serve immediately, garnished with the shredded spring onions.

VARIATION
Wakame is a young, dark-coloured seaweed that can be found dried and in Japanese supermarkets. Nori seaweed could be used instead.

SWEET ADUKI BEAN SOUP WITH RICE CAKES

DON'T ASSUME FROM THE WORD SOUP THAT THIS IS A SAVOURY DISH – ZENZAI IS ACTUALLY A CLASSIC AND POPULAR JAPANESE DESSERT, SERVED WITH THE READY-TO-EAT RICE CAKES (MOCHI) THAT ARE SOLD IN JAPANESE SUPERMARKETS. JAPANESE GREEN TEA MAKES A GOOD ACCOMPANIMENT.

SERVES 4

INGREDIENTS
165g/5^1/$_2$ oz/scant 1 cup dried aduki beans
225g/8oz/1 cup sugar
pinch of salt
4 ready-to-eat rice cakes (mochi)

1 Put the aduki beans in a strainer, wash them under cold running water, then drain them and tip them into a large pan. Add 1 litre/1^3/$_4$ pints/4 cups water and bring to the boil. Drain the aduki beans and return them to the rinsed out pan.

2 Add a further 1.2 litres/2 pints/ 5 cups water to the pan and bring to the boil, then add a further 1.2 litres/ 2 pints/5 cups water and bring to the boil again. Lower the heat and simmer for 30 minutes until the beans are soft.

3 Skim the surface of the broth regularly to remove any scum, if left, it would give the soup an unpleasant bitter taste.

4 When the beans are soft enough to be mashed between your fingers, add half the sugar and simmer for a further 20 minutes.

5 Add the remaining sugar and the salt to the pan, stirring until the sugar has completely dissolved.

6 Heat the grill, then grill both sides of the rice cakes until softened, but not browned. Add the rice cakes to the soup and bring to the boil. Serve the soup immediately in deep warmed bowls.

SIMPLE ROLLED SUSHI

THESE SIMPLE ROLLS, KNOWN AS HOSOMAKI, ARE AN EXCELLENT WAY OF LEARNING THE ART OF ROLLING SUSHI. THEY ARE VERY GOOD FOR PICNICS AND CANAPÉS AND ARE ALWAYS SERVED COLD. YOU WILL NEED A BAMBOO MAT (MAKISU) FOR THE ROLLING PROCESS.

MAKES 12 ROLLS OR 72 SLICES

INGREDIENTS
400g/14oz/2 cups sushi rice, soaked
  for 20 minutes in water to cover
55ml/3½ tbsp rice vinegar
15ml/1 tbsp sugar
2.5ml/½ tsp salt
6 sheets yaki-nori seaweed
200g/7oz tuna, in one piece
200g/7oz salmon, in one piece
wasabi paste
½ cucumber, quartered lengthways
  and seeded
pickled ginger, to garnish (optional)
Japanese soy sauce, to serve

1 Drain the rice, then put in a pan with 525ml/18fl oz/2¼ cups water. Bring to the boil, then lower the heat, cover and simmer for 20 minutes, or until all the liquid has been absorbed. Meanwhile, heat the vinegar, sugar and salt, stir well and cool. Add to the hot rice, then remove the pan from the heat and allow to stand (covered) for 20 minutes.

2 Cut the yaki-nori sheets in half lengthways. Cut the tuna and salmon into four long sticks, each about the same length as the long side of the yaki-nori, and about 1cm/½in square if viewed from the side.

3 Place a sheet of yaki-nori, shiny side down, on a bamboo mat. Divide the rice into 12 portions. Spread one portion over the yaki-nori, leaving a 1cm/½ in clear space at the top and bottom.

4 Spread a little wasabi paste in a horizontal line along the middle of the rice and lay one or two sticks of tuna on this.

5 Holding the mat and the edge of the yaki-nori nearest to you, roll up the yaki-nori and rice into a cylinder with the tuna in the middle. Use the mat as a guide – do not roll it into the food. Roll the rice tightly so that it sticks together and encloses the filling firmly.

6 Carefully roll the sushi off the mat. Make 11 more rolls in the same way, four for each filling ingredient, but do not use wasabi with the cucumber. Use a wet knife to cut each roll into six slices and stand them on a platter. Garnish with pickled ginger, if you wish, and serve with soy sauce.

ASSORTED TEMPURA

TEMPURA IS ONE OF JAPAN'S MOST FAMOUS AND DELICIOUS DISHES. FISH, RATHER THAN MEAT, IS TRADITIONALLY USED, BUT CHOOSE ANY VEGETABLE YOU LIKE. THE ESSENCE OF GOOD TEMPURA IS THAT IT SHOULD BE COOKED AND SERVED IMMEDIATELY.

SERVES 4–6

INGREDIENTS
1 small sweet potato, about 115g/4oz
8 large tiger prawns
1 small squid, cleaned
vegetable oil, for deep frying
flour, for coating
1 small carrot, cut into matchsticks
4 shiitake mushrooms, stems removed
50g/2oz French beans, trimmed
1 red pepper, seeded and sliced into
   2cm/3⁄4in thick strips

For the dip
200ml/7fl oz/scant 1 cup water
45ml/3 tbsp mirin (sweet rice wine)
10g/1⁄4oz bonito flakes
45ml/3 tbsp Japanese soy sauce

For the batter
1 egg
90ml/6 tbsp iced water
75g/3oz/3⁄4 cup plain flour
2.5ml/1⁄2 tsp baking powder
2 ice cubes

2 Peel the prawns, leaving the tail shells intact, and de-vein. Lay a prawn on its side. Make three or four diagonal slits, about two-thirds of the way in towards the spine, leaving all the pieces attached. Repeat with the rest. Flatten with your fingers. Cut the body of the squid into 3cm/1¼in thick strips.

3 Put the egg in a large bowl, stir without beating and set half aside. Add the water, flour and baking powder. Stir two or three times, leaving some flour unblended. Add the ice cubes.

4 Heat the oil in a deep fryer to 185°C/365°F. Dust the prawns lightly with flour. Holding each in turn by the tail, dip them into the batter, then carefully lower them into the hot oil; cook until golden. Fry the remaining prawns and the squid in the same way. Keep warm.

5 Reduce the temperature of the oil to 170°C/340°F. Drain the sweet potato and pat dry. Dip the vegetables into the batter and deep fry (see Cook's Tip). Drain well, then keep warm. As soon as all the tempura are ready, serve with the dip.

1 Mix the dip ingredients in a pan. Bring to the boil, cool, then strain. Divide among 4–6 bowls. Slice the unpeeled sweet potato thinly. Put in a bowl with cold water to cover.

COOK'S TIP
Batter and deep fry the carrots and beans in small bunches. The mushrooms look best if only the undersides are dipped. Cut a cross in the upper side of the mushroom cap, if you like.

GREEN AND YELLOW LAYERED CAKES

THIS COLOURFUL TWO-TONE DESSERT IS MADE BY MOULDING CONTRASTING MIXTURES IN A SMALL POUCH. THE JAPANESE TITLE IS DERIVED FROM THE PREPARATION TECHNIQUE: CHAKIN-SHIBORI, IN WHICH CHAKIN MEANS A POUCH SHAPE AND SHIBORI MEANS A MOULDING ACTION.

MAKES 6

INGREDIENTS
For the yolk mixture (kimi-an)
   6 small hard-boiled eggs
   50g/2oz/¼ cup sugar

For the pea mixture (endo-an)
   200g/7oz/1¾ cups frozen peas
   40g/1½oz/3 tbsp sugar

1 Make the yolk mixture. Shell the eggs, cut them in half and scoop the yolks into a sieve placed over a bowl. Using a wooden spoon, press the yolks through the sieve. Add the sugar and mix well.

2 To make the pea mixture, cook the peas in lightly salted boiling water for about 3–4 minutes, until softened. Drain and place in a mortar, then crush with a pestle. Transfer the paste to a saucepan. Add the sugar and cook over a low heat until thick. Stir constantly so that the mixture does not burn.

3 Spread out the pea paste in a shallow dish so that it cools as quickly as possible. Divide both mixtures into six portions.

COOK'S TIP
Use a food processor instead of a mortar and pestle if preferred. Process for a few seconds to make a coarse paste.

4 Wet a piece of muslin or thin cotton and wring it out well. Place a portion of the pea mixture on the cloth and put a similar amount of the yolk mixture on top. Wrap the mixture up and twist the top of the cloth to join the mixtures together and mark a spiral pattern on the top. Unwrap and place on a plate. Make five more cakes in the same way. Serve cold.

SUKIYAKI

YOU WILL NEED A SPECIAL CAST-IRON SUKIYAKI PAN (SUKIYAKI-NABE) AND BURNER OR A SIMILAR TABLE-TOP COOKER FOR THIS DISH. IT IS GREAT FUN BECAUSE GUESTS CAN COOK THEIR OWN DINNER IN FRONT OF THEM, AND THEN HELP THEMSELVES TO THE DELICIOUS MORSELS OF FOOD.

SERVES 4

INGREDIENTS
  1kg/2¼lb beef topside, thinly sliced
  lard, for cooking
  4 leeks or spring onions, sliced
    diagonally into 1cm/½in pieces
  bunch of shungiku leaves, stems
    removed, chopped (optional)
  bunch of enoki mushrooms, brown
    roots cut off (optional)
  8 shiitake mushrooms, stems
    removed
  300g/11oz shirataki noodles, boiled
    for 2 minutes, drained and halved
  2 pieces grilled beancurd (yaki tofu),
    about 10 × 7cm/4 × 2¾in, cut into
    3cm/1¼in cubes
  4 fresh eggs, to serve

For the sukiyaki stock
  100ml/3½fl oz/scant ½ cup mirin
    (sweet rice wine)
  45ml/3 tbsp sugar
  105ml/7 tbsp Japanese soy sauce

For the seasoning mix
  200ml/7fl oz/scant 1 cup dashi
    (kombu and bonito stock) or
    instant dashi
  100ml/3½fl oz/scant ½ cup sake or
    dry white wine
  15ml/1 tbsp Japanese soy sauce

1 Make the sukiyaki stock. Pour the mirin (sweet rice wine) into a pan and bring to the boil. Stir in the sugar and soy sauce, bring to the boil, then remove from the heat and set aside.

2 To make the seasoning mix, heat the dashi, sake or wine and soy sauce in a small pan. As soon as the mixture boils, remove from the heat and set aside.

3 Fan out the beef slices on a large serving plate. Put the lard for cooking on the same plate. Arrange all the remaining ingredients, except the eggs, on one or more large plates.

4 Stand the portable cooker on a suitably heavy mat to protect the dining table and ensure that it can be heated safely. Melt the lard, add three or four slices of beef and some leeks or spring onions, and then pour in the sukiyaki stock. Gradually add the remaining ingredients, except the eggs.

5 Place each egg in a ramekin and beat lightly with chopsticks. Place one before each diner. When the beef and vegetables are cooked, diners help themselves to whatever they fancy, dipping their chosen piece of meat, vegetable or grilled beancurd (yaki tofu) in the raw egg before eating.

6 When the stock has thickened, gradually stir in the seasoning mix and carry on cooking until all the ingredients have been eaten.

CHAP CHAE

A Korean stir-fry of mixed vegetables and noodles garnished attractively with the yellow and white egg shapes that are so typically Korean.

SERVES 4

INGREDIENTS
  225g/8oz rump or sirloin steak
  115g/4oz cellophane noodles, soaked
    for 20 minutes in hot water to cover
  4 Chinese dried mushrooms, soaked
    for 30 minutes in warm water
  groundnut oil, for stir-frying
  2 eggs, separated
  1 carrot, cut into matchsticks
  1 onion, sliced
  2 courgettes or ½ cucumber, cut
    into sticks
  ½ red pepper, seeded and cut
    into strips
  4 button mushrooms, sliced
  75g/3oz/1½ cups beansprouts,
    washed and drained
  15ml/1 tbsp light soy sauce
  salt and ground black pepper
  sliced spring onions and sesame
    seeds, to garnish

1 Put the steak in the freezer until it is firm enough to cut into thin slices and then into 5cm/2in strips.

2 Mix the ingredients for the marinade in a shallow dish (see Cook's Tip), stir in the steak strips. Drain the noodles and cook them in boiling water for 5 minutes. Drain again, then snip into short lengths. Drain the mushrooms, cut off and discard the stems; slice the caps.

3 Prepare the garnish. Heat the oil in a small frying pan. Beat the egg yolks together and pour into the pan. When set, slide them on to a plate. Add the egg whites to the pan and cook until set. Cut both yolks and whites into diamond shapes and set aside.

COOK'S TIP
To make the marinade, blend together 15ml/1 tbsp sugar, 30ml/2 tbsp light soy sauce, 45ml/3 tbsp sesame oil, 4 finely chopped spring onions, 1 crushed garlic clove and 10ml/2 tsp crushed toasted sesame seeds.

4 Drain the beef. Heat the oil in a wok or large frying pan and stir-fry the beef until it changes colour. Add the carrot and onion and stir-fry for 2 minutes, then add the other vegetables, tossing them until just cooked.

5 Add the noodles and season with soy sauce, salt and pepper. Cook for 1 minute. Spoon into a serving dish and garnish with egg, spring onions and sesame seeds.

KIMCHI

No self-respecting Korean moves far without the beloved Kimchi. In the past, large stone pots were filled with this pickled cabbage, and buried in the ground for the winter.

SERVES 6–8

INGREDIENTS
  675g/1½lb Chinese leaves, shredded
  1 large or 2 medium yam beans,
    total weight about 675g/1½lb or
    2 hard pears, peeled and thinly
    sliced
  60ml/4 tbsp salt
  200ml/7fl oz/scant 1 cup water
  4 spring onions, finely chopped
  4 garlic cloves, crushed
  2.5cm/1in piece fresh root ginger,
    peeled and finely chopped
  10–15ml/2–3 tsp chilli powder

1 Place the Chinese leaves and yam beans or pears in a bowl and sprinkle evenly with salt. Mix well, then press down into the bowl.

2 Pour the water over the vegetables, then cover the bowl and leave overnight in a cool place. Next day, drain off the brine from the vegetables and set it aside. Mix the brined vegetables with the spring onions, garlic, ginger and chilli powder (use rubber gloves if you have sensitive hands). Pack the mixture into a 900g/2lb jar or two smaller ones. Pour over the reserved brine.

3 Cover with clear film and place on a sunny window-sill or in an airing cupboard for 2–3 days. Thereafter store in the fridge, where the mixture can be kept for several weeks.

MARINATED BEEF STEAKS

BULGOGI IS A VERY POPULAR DISH FOR OUTDOOR ENTERTAINING. TRADITIONALLY IT WOULD HAVE BEEN COOKED ON A GENGHIS KHAN GRILL, WHICH IS SHAPED LIKE THE CROWN OF A HAT, BUT A RIDGED HEAVY FRYING PAN OR WOK WORKS ALMOST AS WELL.

SERVES 3–4

INGREDIENTS
   450g/1lb fillet of beef or rump
     steak, in the piece
   sesame oil, for frying

For the marinade
   150ml/¼ pint/⅔ cup dark soy sauce
   30ml/2 tbsp sesame oil
   30ml/2 tbsp sake or dry white wine
   1 garlic clove, cut into thin slivers
   15ml/1 tbsp sugar
   30ml/2 tbsp crushed roasted
     sesame seeds
   4 spring onions, cut into long lengths
   salt and ground black pepper

1 Put the meat into the freezer until it is firm enough to slice very thinly and evenly. Arrange the slices of beef in a shallow glass dish.

2 Make the marinade. Mix the soy sauce, oil, sake or wine, garlic, sugar and sesame seeds in a bowl and add the spring onions. Season to taste.

3 Pour the marinade over the slices of beef and mix well. Cover the dish and transfer to the fridge. Chill for at least 3 hours or overnight.

4 Heat the merest slick of oil in a ridged heavy frying pan or wok. Drain the beef slices and fry over a high heat for a few seconds, turning once. Serve at once.

PORK AND SPRING ONION PANCAKES

BINDAEDUK *IS SOMETIMES REFERRED TO AS* KOREA'S *ANSWER TO THE PIZZA, ALTHOUGH IT IS REALLY A BEANCAKE. THE FILLING CAN INCLUDE* KIMCHI (*PICKLED CABBAGE*), *CARROT AND GINGER, BUT PORK AND SPRING ONIONS ARE MORE TRADITIONAL INGREDIENTS.*

2 Add the soy sauce, sesame seeds and bicarbonate of soda and process briefly to mix. When ready to cook, tip the batter into a bowl and add the beansprouts, garlic, spring onions and pork. Season to taste.

3 Heat about 10ml/2 tsp of the sesame oil in a large frying pan. Spoon or ladle in half the batter, and, using the back of a spoon, spread it into a thick pancake.

SERVES 4–6

INGREDIENTS
   225g/8oz/1¼ cups skinned, split
     mung beans
   50g/2oz/⅓ cup glutinous rice
   15ml/1 tbsp light soy sauce
   15ml/1 tbsp roasted sesame
     seeds, crushed
   2.5ml/½ tsp bicarbonate of soda
   115g/4oz/½ cup beansprouts,
     blanched and dried
   1 garlic clove, crushed
   4 spring onions, chopped
   115g/4oz cooked lean pork, shredded
   30ml/2 tbsp sesame oil, plus extra
     for drizzling
   salt and ground black pepper
   fresh chives, to garnish
   light soy sauce, to serve

1 Pick over the mung beans and put them in a bowl. Add the glutinous rice and pour in water to cover. Leave to soak for at least 8 hours. After this time, tip the beans and rice into a sieve, rinse under cold water, then drain. Put the mixture into a food processor and process to a batter with the consistency of double cream.

4 Drizzle a little more sesame oil over the surface of the pancake, cover and cook over a medium heat until the underside is cooked. Invert a lightly oiled plate over the pan. Remove the pan from the heat and, holding both plate and pan tightly together, turn both over carefully so that the pancake is transferred to the plate. Slide it back into the pan and cook on the other side for 3–4 minutes more. Keep this first pancake hot while cooking a second pancake in the same way. Place the pancakes on serving plates and garnish with chives. Cut into wedges and serve with soy sauce.

SHOPPING FOR ASIAN FOODS

UK

Chinese

Good Harvest
   Fish Market
14 Newport Place
London WC2H 7PR
Tel: 020 7437 0712

Golden Gate
   Cake Shop
13 Macclesfield Street
London W1V 7LH
Tel: 020 7287 9862

Golden Gate Supermarket
16 Newport Place
London WC2H 7JS
Tel: 020 7437 6266

Golden Gate
   Hong Kong Ltd
14 Lisle Street
London WC2 7BE
Tel: 020 7437 0014

Hong Kong Supermarket
62 High Street
London SW4 7UL
Tel: 020 7720 2069

Loon Fung Supermarket
42–44 Gerrard Street
London W1V 7LP
Tel: 020 7437 7332

New Peking Supermarket
59 Westbourne Grove
London W2 4UA
Tel: 020 7928 8770

Newport Supermarket
28–29 Newport Court
London WC2H 7PQ
Tel: 020 7437 2386

Rum Wong Supermarket
London Road
Guildford
Surrey GU1 2AF
Tel: 01483 451 568

S. W. Trading Ltd
Horn Lane
Greenwich
London SE10 0RT
Tel: 020 8293 9393

Wang Thai Supermarket
101 Kew Road
Richmond
Surrey TW9 2PN
Tel: 020 8332 2959

The Wing On Department
   Store (Hong Kong) Ltd
37–38 Margaret Street
London W1N 7FA
Tel: 020 7580 3677

Wing Tai
11a Aylesham Centre
Rye Lane
London SE15 5EW
Tel: 020 7635 0714

Wing Yip
395 Edgware Road
London NW2 6LN
Tel: 020 7450 0422

also at
Oldham Road
Ancoats
Manchester
M4 5HU
Tel: 0161 832 3215

and
375 Nechells Park Road
Nechells
Birmingham
B7 5NT
Tel: 0121 327 3838

South-east Asian

Hopewell Emporium
2f Dyne Road
London NW6 7XB
Tel: 020 7624 5473

Manila Supermarket
11–12 Hogarth Place
London SW5 0QT
Tel: 020 7373 8305

Miah, A. and Co
20 Magdalen Street
Norwich NR3 1HE
Tel: 01603 615395

Sri Thai
56 Shepherd's Bush Road
London W6 7PH
Tel: 020 7602 0621

Talad Thai Ltd
320 Upper Richmond Road
London SW15 6TL
Tel: 020 8789 8084

Tawana
18–20 Chepstow Road
London W2 5BD
Tel: 020 7221 6316

Japanese

Arigato
48–50 Brewer Street
London W1R 3HM
Tel: 020 7287 1722

Miura Japanese Foods
44 Coombe Road
Nr Kingston KT2 7AF
Tel: 020 8549 8076

also at
5 Limpsfield Road
Sanderstead
Surrey CR2 9LA
Tel: 020 8651 4498

Natural House
Japan Centre
212 Piccadilly
London W1V 9LD
Tel: 020 7434 4218

Oriental City
399 Edgware Road
London NW9 0JJ
Tel: 020 8200 0009

T.K. Trading
Unit 6/7
The Chase Centre
Chase Road
London NW10 6QD
Tel: 020 8453 1001

Thai

Rum Wong Supermarket
London Road
Guildford
Surrey GU1 2AF
Tel: 01483 451568

Talad Thai Ltd
320 Upper Richmond Road
London SW15 6TL
Tel: 020 8789 8084

Tawana Supermarket
18 Chepstow Road
London W2 4BD
Tel: 020 7221 6316

Equipment

Neal Street East
5–7 Neal Street
London WC2 9PV
Tel: 020 7240 0135

Obhrai Cash and Carry
168 Ealing Road
Wembley
Middlesex HA0 4DQ
Tel: 020 8903 4450

Popat Store
138 Ealing Road
Wembley
Middlesex HA0 4PY
Tel: 020 8903 6797

Mail Order Companies

Fiddes Payne Herbs and
Spices Ltd
Unit 3B, Thorpe Way
Banbury
Oxfordshire OX16 8XL
Tel: 01295 253 888

Fox's Spices
Mason's Road
Stratford-upon-Avon
Warwickshire CV37 9XN
Tel: 01789 266 420

General Information

Bart's Spices
York Road
Bedminster
Bristol BS3 4AD
Tel: 0117 977 3474
Fax: 0117 972 0216

Fiddes Payne Herbs and
Spices Ltd
Unit 3B, Thorpe Way
Banbury
Oxfordshire OX16 8XL
Tel: 01295 253 888

Sharwood's Ethnic
Food Bureau
Nexus Choat
Bury House
126–128 Cromwell Road
London SW7 4ET
Tel: 020 7373 4537

AUSTRALIA

Asian Supermarkets
Pty Ltd
116 Charters Towers Road
Townsville
QLD 4810
Tel: (07) 4772 3997
Fax: (07) 4771 3919

PK Supermarkets Pty Ltd
369 Victoria Avenue
Chatswood
NSW 2067
Tel: (02) 9419 8822

Kongs Trading Pty Ltd
8 Kingscote Street
Kewdale
WA 6105
Tel: (08) 9353 3380
Fax: (08) 9353 3390

Duc Hung Long Asian
Foodstore
95 The Crescent
Fairfield
NSW 2165
Tel: (02) 9728 1092

Exotic Asian Groceries
Q Supercentre
Cnr Market and Bermuda
Streets
Mermaid Waters
QLD 4218
Tel: (07) 5572 8188

Saigon Asian Food Retail
and Wholesale
6 Cape Street
Dickson
ACT 2602
Tel: (02) 6247 4251

The Spice and Herb
Asian Shop
200 Old Cleveland Road
Capalaba
QLD 4157
Tel: (07) 3245 5300

Sydney Fish Market Pty Ltd
Cnr Pyrmont Bridge Road and
Bank Street
Pyrmont
NSW 2009
Tel: (02) 9660 1611

Harris Farm Markets
Sydney Markets
Flemongton
NSW 2140
Tel: (02) 9746 2055
(Also in QLD, plus
suburban stores)

Burlington Supermarkets
Chinatown Mall
Fortitude Valley
QLD 4006
Tel: (07) 3216 1828

Author's Acknowledgements

Sallie Morris would like to thank her family: Johnnie, Alex and James for their support; Beryl Castles for her help in typing the manuscript; Beth Walter for advice on recipes from the Philippines; Rupert Welchman for his advice on Japanese recipes; John Phengsiri at the Wang Thai Supermarket in Richmond; Bart's Spices Ltd; Cherry Valley Farms (Tel: 01472 371 271), who supplied ducklings for recipe testing; Ken the Fishman from Grimsby (Tel: 0860 240 213), and Magimix (Tel: 01483 427 411) for supplying a food processor, ice cream maker and electric steamer for recipe testing.

Deh-ta Hsiung would like to thank Sallie Morris and Emi Kazuko for their advice and help in writing about South-east Asian and Japanese foods.

INDEX

A

acar bening, 86
adobo of chicken and pork, 102
aduki beans: sweet aduki bean soup with rice cakes, 114
Anita Wong's duck, 22
apples: Chinese honeyed apples, 18
asparagus and crab soup, 98
asparagus beans see green beans
aubergines: laksa lemak, 40
    Sichuan spiced aubergine, 26

B

bamboo shoots, red chicken curry with, 70
bamie goreng, 91
banana fritters, 92
bang bang chicken, 28
basil: stir-fried chicken with basil and chilli, 66
bawang goreng, 88
bean thread vermicelli see cellophane noodles
beancurd: crispy Shanghai spring rolls, 20
    Indian mee goreng, 57
    laksa lemak, 40
    miso soup, 114
    Mongolian firepot, 16
    steamboat, 45
beansprouts: egg foo yung – Cantonese style, 30

Filipino prawn fritters, 100
thamin lethok, 77
Vietnamese rice paper rolls, 96
beef: rendang, 88
    Cantonese fried noodles, 31
    chap chae, 120
    marinated beef steaks, 122
    Mussaman curry, 72
    nasi goreng, 83
    sizzling steak, 46
    spicy meat balls, 84
    spicy shredded beef, 33
    steamboat, 45
    sukiyaki, 119
bindaeduk, 123
bread rolls: ensaimadas, 105
bubor pulot hitam, 92
bulgogi, 122
buns see steamed buns
Burmese recipes, 76–7

C

cahn cua, 98
Cantonese recipes, 29–32
cellophane noodles: chap chae, 120
    Thai spring rolls, 60
cha shao, 53
chao gio, 97
chap chae, 120
chick-peas: puchero, 104
chicken: adobo of chicken and pork, 102
    bamie goreng, 91
    bang bang chicken, 28
    barbecued chicken, 69

chicken and egg with rice, 112
chicken rendang, 43
chicken satay, 42
chicken, vegetable and chilli salad, 98
drunken chicken, 13
ginger, chicken and coconut soup, 64
lettuce parcels, 37
nasi goreng, 83
puchero, 104
red chicken curry with bamboo shoots, 70
Sichuan chicken with kung po sauce, 24
steamboat, 45
stir-fried chicken with basil and chilli, 66
yakitori chicken, 111
chillies: chicken, vegetable and chilli salad, 98
    chilli crabs, 54
    chilli sambal, 84
    stir-fried chicken with basil and chilli, 66
Chinese hot pot see Mongolian firepot
Chinese leaves: kimchi, 120
Chinese recipes, 12-32
Chinese sausages, congee with Chinese sausage, 36
    popiah, 50
chow mein, 31
churros, 106
clams: laksa lemak, 40
coconut milk and cream:
    Balinese vegetable soup, 81
    black glutinous rice pudding, 92
    curried prawns in coconut milk, 73
    fish moolie, 44
    ginger, chicken and coconut soup, 64
    laksa lemak, 40
    Malaysian coconut ice cream, 48
    stewed pumpkin in coconut cream, 74
coconut chips, 49
cod: fish cakes with cucumber relish, 63
    mohinga, 76
    sinigang, 103

congee with Chinese sausage, 36
corn cobs: baby, ginger, chicken and coconut soup, 64
cucumber: bang bang chicken, 28
    fish cakes with cucumber relish, 63
    fruit and raw vegetable gado-gado, 87
    Peking duck with mandarin pancakes, 14
    sambal nanas, 56
    sweet and sour salad, 86
crabs: asparagus and crab soup, 98
    chao gio, 97
    chilli crabs, 54
    crisp-fried crabs claws, 62
    popiah, 50
cucumbers: fish cakes with cucumber relish, 63
    sambal nanas, 56
cumi cumi smoor, 82
curries: curried prawns in coconut milk, 73
    fish moolie, 44
    Mussaman curry, 72
    red chicken curry with bamboo shoots, 70

D

desserts: banana fritters, 92
    black glutinous rice pudding, 92
    Chinese honeyed apples, 18
    green and yellow layered cakes, 118
    iced fruit mountain, 18
    leche flan, 106
    Malaysian coconut ice cream, 48
    mangoes with sticky rice, 74
    stewed pumpkin in coconut cream, 74
dim sum: pork-stuffed steamed buns, 34
    steamed flower rolls, 34
drunken chicken, 13
duck: Anita Wong's, 22
    duck breasts with pineapple and ginger, 32
    Peking duck with mandarin pancakes, 14
dumplings see steamed buns

E
East China recipes, 20–2
egg rolls
 see spring rolls
eggs: chicken and egg with
  rice, 112
  egg foo yung – Cantonese
   style, 30
  fruit and vegetable gado-
   gado, 87
  green and yellow layered
   cakes, 118
  leche flan, 106
  popiah, 50
  steamboat, 45
  stuffed Thai omelettes, 68
  tea eggs, 22
ensaimadas, 105
escabeche, 101

F
fish: *escabeche*, 101
  fish cakes with cucumber
   relish, 63
  fish moolie, 44
  mohingha, 76
  sinigang, 103
  steamboat, 45
fritters: banana, 92
  Chinese honeyed
   apples, 18
  churros, 106
  Filipino prawn, 100
fruit: and raw vegetable
   gado-gado, 87
  iced fruit mountain, 18
  sweet and sour
   salad, 86
  see also individual types
   e.g. apples

G
gado-gado: fruit and raw
  vegetable, 87
ginger, duck breasts with pineapple and, 32
glass noodles *see* cellophane
  noodles
glutinous rice: black glutinous
  rice pudding, 92
  mangoes with sticky
   rice, 74
goi tom, 98
green beans:
  Balinese vegetable
   soup, 81
  kan shao green
   beans, 26

H
haddock: *sinigang*, 103
Hong Kong recipes, 33–7
hosomaki, 116
hot and sour prawn soup, 64
hot and sour soup, 12

I
ice cream: Malaysian
  coconut, 48
Indian *mee goreng*, 57
Indonesian recipes, 80–92

J
Japanese recipes, 110-9

K
kan shao green beans, 26
kimchi, 120
Korean recipes, 120–3

L
laksa lemak, 40
lamb: hot and sour soup, 12
  lamb saté, 80
  Mongolian firepot, 16
leche flan, 106
lettuce parcels, 37
lion's head meat balls, 21

M
Malaysian recipes, 40–9
mandarin pancakes, 14
mangoes with sticky rice, 74
meats: spicy meat balls, 84
  see also beef; chicken;
   duck; lamb; pork
mee goreng, Indian, 57
melon: iced fruit
  mountain, 18
miso soup, 114
mohingha, 76
Mongolian firepot, 16
mung bean noodles *see*
  cellophane noodles
mung beans: pork and spring
  onion pancakes, 123
mushrooms: crispy Shanghai
  spring rolls, 20
  hot and sour soup, 12
  steamboat, 45
  Thai spring rolls, 60
Mussaman curry, 72

N
nasi goreng, 83
nonya pork satay, 54
noodles: *bamie goreng*, 91

Cantonese fried noodles, 31
chap chae, 120
fruit and raw vegetable
  gado-gado, 87
Indian *mee goreng*, 57
laksa lemak, 40
Sichuan noodles with
  sesame sauce, 25
sukiyaki, 119
Thai spring rolls, 60
thamin lethok, 77
North China recipes, 12-18
nuoc cham sauce, 97

O
omelettes: egg foo yung –
  Cantonese style, 30
  stuffed Thai
   omelettes, 68
onigiri, 113
onions, deep-fried, 88
oyako-don, 112

P
pancake rolls
 see spring rolls
pancakes: mandarin, 14
  pork and spring
   onion, 123
papayas: green papaya
  salad, 67
pawpaws *see* papayas
peas: green and yellow layered
  cakes, 118
Peking recipes, 12-18
pergedel djawa, 84
Philippine recipes, 100–6
pineapples: duck breasts

with pineapple and
  ginger, 32
fruit and raw vegetable
  gado-gado, 87
sambal nanas, 56
sweet and sour
  salad, 86
pisang goreng, 92
popiah, 50
pork: adobo of chicken and
  pork, 102
  bamie goreng, 91
  barbecued pork, 53
  Cantonese fried
   noodles, 31
  chao gio, 97
  crispy Shanghai
   rolls, 20
  hot and sour soup, 12
  lion's head meat
   balls, 21
  nasi goreng, 83

nonya pork satay, 54
popiah, 50
pork and spring onion
  pancakes, 123
pork-stuffed steamed
  buns, 34
puchero, 104
steamboat, 45
stuffed Thai omelettes, 68
Thai spring rolls, 60
Vietnamese rice paper
  rolls, 96
potatoes: beef rendang, 88
tempura, assorted, 117
thamin lethok, 77

poultry *see* chicken; duck
prawns: *bamie goreng*, 91
  crispy Shanghai spring
    rolls, 20
  curried prawns in coconut
    milk, 73
  Filipino prawn fritters, 100
  hot and sour prawn
    soup, 64
  laksa lemak, 40
  nasi goreng, 83
  popiah, 50
  sambal goreng with
    prawns, 90
  sinigang, 103
  steamboat, 45
  tempura, assorted, 117
  Thai spring rolls, 60
  Vietnamese rice paper
    rolls, 96
puchero, 104
puddings *see* desserts
pumpkin: stewed pumpkin
  in coconut cream, 74

R
rendang: beef, 88
  chicken, 43
rice: black glutinous rice
    pudding, 92
  chicken and egg with
    rice, 112
  compressed rice
    shapes, 80
  congee with Chinese
    sausage, 36
  mangoes with sticky
    rice, 74
  nasi goreng, 83
  pork and spring onion
    pancakes, 123
  rice triangles, 113
  simple rolled
    sushi, 116
  thamin lethok, 77
rice cakes, sweet aduki bean
  soup with, 114
rice papers: Vietnamese rice
  paper rolls, 96
rice vermicelli: steamboat, 45
  Vietnamese rice paper
    rolls, 96

S
salads: chicken, vegetable and
    chilli, 98
  green papaya, 67
  sweet and sour , 86

salmon: rice triangles, 113
  sashimi, 110
  simple rolled sushi, 116
sambals: chilli sambal, 84
  sambal goreng with
    prawns, 90
  sambal nanas, 56
  sotong sambal, 47
samosas, 52
sang choy, 37
sashimi, 110
satays: chicken, 42
  nonya pork, 54
satés: lamb saté, 80
sausages *see* Chinese
    sausages
scallions *see* spring onions
sesame paste: Sichuan
    noodles with sesame
    sauce, 25
Shanghai recipes, 20–2
shellfish *see* types of shellfish
    e.g. crabs
shrimps: *sambal nanas*, 56
  see also prawns
Sichuan recipes, 24–8
Singapore recipes, 50–7
sinigang, 103
sotong sambal, 47
soups: asparagus and crab, 98
  Balinese vegetable, 81
  crispy wonton, 29
  ginger, chicken and
    coconut, 64
  hot and sour, 12
  hot and sour prawn, 64
  laksa lemak, 40
  miso, 114
  puchero, 104
  sweet aduki bean soup with
    rice cakes, 114
South China recipes, 29-32
spring onions: pork and spring
  onion pancakes, 123
spring rolls: *chao gio*, 97
  crispy Shanghai, 20
  popiah, 50
  Thai, 60
  Vietnamese rice paper
    rolls, 96
squid: assorted tempura, 117
  sotong sambal, 47
  spicy squid, 82
steak *see* beef
steamboat, 45
steamed buns: pork-
    stuffed, 34
  steamed flower rolls, 34

stir-fried dishes: chicken with
    basil and chilli, 66
sukiyaki, 119
sushi: simple rolled sushi, 116
sweet potatoes: assorted
    tempura, 117
sweet rice *see* glutinous
    rice
sweet and sour salad, 86

T
tea eggs, 22
tempura, assorted, 117
Thai beans *see* green beans
Thai recipes, 64–74
thamin lethok, 77
tofu *see* beancurd
tom yam kung, 64
transparent noodles *see*
    cellophane noodles
tuna: simple rolled
    sushi, 116

U
ukoy, 100

V
vegetables: Balinese vegetable
    soup, 81
  chap chae, 120
  chicken, vegetable and
    chilli salad, 98
  fruit and raw vegetable
    gado-gado, 87
  see also individual types
    e.g. asparagus
Vietnamese recipes, 96–8

Vietnamese rice paper
    rolls, 96

W
waxy rice *see* glutinous rice
West China recipes, 24–8
wind-dried sausages *see*
    Chinese sausages
wontons: crispy wonton
    soup, 29

Y
yakitori chicken, 111
yard-long beans *see*
    green beans

Z
zenzai, 114